Contents

Contents continued overleaf

Contents

STAFF AND EDUCATIONAL DEVELOPMENT ASSOCIATI

e-Teaching:
Engaging Learners
Through Technology

tock FSEDA

ark Schofield

Preface

The technology available in Further and Higher Education in the UK has been developing rapidly and the previous SEDA paper on the subject had inevitably dated (O'Hagan, 1997). It was time for a new guide to using technology for teaching and supporting learning, and I seemed to be in a position to write it. I have used computers and other technologies for 25 years in my own teaching in UK universities, and I have spent much of the last five years discussing with other teachers how they might use it. I hope this book will be of use to those who are starting to teach in F/HE, or starting to teach with technology.

The title of this publication caused me some reflection. 'E-learning' is the current official term, and it marks a welcome emphasis on student-centredness. Those of us who have used 'learning technology' for some years must be sanguine about its occasional re-badging. I must admit to the ubiquitous 'e' prefix grating somewhat, because it harks back to the older term 'e-commerce' (Bostock, 2005), which is entirely the wrong model for education - do we want people buying degrees online? I hope not. However, accepting the prefix, as we must, this book is not directly about student learning, it is primarily about teaching, broadly understood as everything that supports student learning, whether face-to-face or online. This will include roles such as lecturer, instructor, demonstrator, task-setter, supporter of learning skills, supervisor, moderator, assessor, and so on. There are few aspects of being a teacher in F/HE that cannot be supported by technology. So, 'e-teaching' reasserts our responsibility as teachers for the design and support of student learning experiences, whether face-to-face or online.

Why should you use technology in teaching? Because, like other ways of teaching and supporting learning, it can be effective and even be fun. To illustrate that, here are three quick personal examples. In 1981, I had one of the early microcomputers and wrote programmes for it, including statistical analyses. On a one-day extramural course with mature students, I was able to teach a topic in quantitative ecology by having them collect field data and then immediately use our computer to analyse the data statistically and display the results graphically. Discussion of theory followed naturally. The computer transformed the way I could teach the subject. Secondly, in 1995, I taught my first Web-based course, with about 200 students. Walking around a PC laboratory to watch three dozen students working with my Web pages was a thrill, and their evaluations told me they preferred it to my lectures! Thirdly and most recently, I have helped colleagues use voting technology in their lectures. It has been impressive to watch *all* students immediately answer questions by voting, and get immediate feedback from the lecturer on their answers. At the end of a lecture students are asked to vote on whether they want to use the technology again. The response is usually overwhelmingly positive; real progress within the ancient tradition of the lecture.

Why should you use a technology in teaching? We could ask the equally difficult question, why are you teaching the way you currently do? Educational technology is a Trojan horse: inside are some fundamental questions about teaching and student learning, ready to break out and open the city walls to some radical changes in practice (see Chickering and Ehrmann, 1996). Rising to that challenge is as intriguing as anything in teaching.

I have referred occasionally in the text to named software. This is not an endorsement; there are often several examples that could have been given but there is no space for a complete list or a software review. You may have access to, or prefer, different software. The same principles will apply and you should seek the advice of local experts on the details. Although the book is predominantly about computer-based technology, some non-electronic teaching aids are included as they need to be considered alongside, as alternatives. There is, inevitably, some jargon, which I have usually explained on first use. Further explanations can usually be found on Wikipedia (http://en.wikipedia.org/). A Web site supporting this book is at http://www.keele.org.uk/e-t/.

I am pleased to thank Bob Rotheram (Senior Learning and Teaching Adviser, Nottingham Trent University) for many helpful comments on a draft; any errors are mine.

Stephen Bostock

stephen@keele.org.uk

Dr Stephen Bostock FSEDA has taught with computers in UK universities since 1978. After a first career as a biologist, he taught and managed adult education courses. From the mid-1980s he taught IT courses inside and outside the university, and then moved to a computer science department. From there he developed himself further as an academic developer, and in 2007 he became Head of the Learning Development Unit at Keele University, UK.

1 Introduction

1.1 Why read this book?

Why do you need to know about the uses of technology in teaching and student learning? Before answering the question, let's be clear that you already know quite a lot about educational technologies. You will undoubtedly have encountered, as a student or teacher, some traditional technologies such as a chalkboard or whiteboard, paper handouts or an overhead projector. In the last 25 years or so, such traditional technologies have been supplemented with, or replaced by, computer-based technologies. You probably use e-mail and the World Wide Web. *E-learning* is the current term (in a long line of terms) for any uses of computers and their networks to support teaching and learning. It includes a widening range of applications, for example, simulations and multimedia for students to use independently, digital presentations, and electronic voting for teachers to use in lectures. The Web has become ubiquitous since the mid-1990s; most students use it, although not necessarily well. Some institutions use it to provide wholly online courses (through the Internet). Students commonly use wireless networks and mobile computing (e.g. laptop computers, mobile phones, personal digital assistants, handheld computers), and online virtual learning environments (VLEs).

The reasons to consider using technology (see Teacher Training Agency 1998 in Kennewell 2001, p.106) include providing both students and teachers with:

• Increased speed, capacity and range of access to information

• Automatic processing of data

• Ease of amendment of work, supporting incremental improvement, and

• Immediate feedback on student learning.

When carefully chosen and appropriately used, technology can improve the learning experience, or the cost/effectiveness of its outcomes, or the efficiency of the process. Learning and teaching can be better and/or cheaper; and cheaper may mean saving you time.

This book is an introduction to the types of technology you may find useful in teaching and/or supporting learning in Higher Education. It introduces the technologies and discusses their characteristics, their affordances (utility) and limitations, so that you can make informed decisions about using them. Your local teaching context may offer only some of them, but we can be confident that many computer-based learning and teaching aids will become common. UK Universities are increasingly technology-rich environments and most students find this natural. Some of them capture digital images or videos with their mobile phones; they use e-mail routinely and text 'chat' to friends over the Internet; they routinely use the Web to find resources for learning; and they use a word processor for academic writing. Most of us use new technologies as they come along to enhance aspects of our personal lives; your teaching is no exception.

1.2 Blended learning

'several authors have found that the most efficient teaching model is a blended approach, which combines self-paced learning, live e-learning, and face-to-face classroom learning'
(Alonso *et al.*, 2005, p.234)

I am not suggesting that you should abandon, or even necessarily reduce, your face-to-face contact with students: at most universities, students want personal contact with teachers and you probably enjoy it too (e.g. Monteith and Smith, 2000). Rather, both traditional and technology-supported teaching must pay their way in terms of student learning. We should use them as deliberate choices, rather than teach because that is how we were taught, or because that is how someone else taught the course last year.

This approach to employing educational technology has been termed 'blended learning' - designing a blend of traditional and technology-based teaching and learning activities. Every teaching and learning situation is different, and the optimum blend may be technology-rich or technology-lite. We owe it to ourselves and to our students to be aware of the technologies available, their utilities and limitations, so that we can 'mix and match' our teaching methods and our technologies. An awareness of what is possible with a technology available to you may prompt you to try it, to address a problem or an opportunity in your own teaching. 'Nothing ventured, nothing gained.' Here are some scenarios based on personal experience:

1   A teacher has several dyslexic students in a class, who need access to lecture notes ahead of lectures. If the notes are written in a word processor (e.g. MS Word) or presentation manager (e.g. PowerPoint), they can be printed a week ahead and distributed, or placed on a course Web site for reading in whatever way individual students prefer

2   A course doubles in student numbers so that the weekly tutorials become impossible within the constraints of rooms and timetables. One solution is to have tutorials in alternate weeks, with discussions continuing in an online, asynchronous text 'discussion board'

3   Third level dissertations are restricted in subject area because of the availability of research journals in the library. Electronic journals and the Web sites of other universities, conferences and research institutes can make a wider literature accessible, especially if links to them are collected on the course Web site

4   A large, mixed-ability first-year course on basic science has a lecture attendance that declines through the semester, with predictable results in the final examination. Formative and summative (for a final grade) multiple choice tests in a virtual learning environment may keep students engaged and give them feedback on their progress, at least in relation to the simpler learning outcomes. The activity monitoring in the VLE allows a teacher to detect which students are failing the tests, or not taking them, so that they can be contacted before they fall behind or drop out.

1.3 An organising framework

Choosing the best technologies to blend with some traditional teaching methods is not simple; there is no blueprint. It involves selecting a technology and designing how it is to be used. Any one technology often has multiple affordances - the possible ways it could be used - depending on the context. A simplified course development process would be:

1   List the student learning activities needed to achieve the intended learning outcomes

2   Select the teaching method or delivery medium or technology to support each learning activity (the blend)

3   Refine the blend for compatibility, balance and cost.

The components of a course can be called teaching-learning activities (TLAs, Biggs, 2003), or pedagogical techniques (Paulsen, 1995), each consisting of a learning activity and its support. In an imaginary course, an example list of learning activities and their traditional supporting methods is suggested in Figure 1. One or more of these methods, or 'media' (Laurillard, 2002), could be replaced with advantage by a technology-based activity (in the adjacent column). Or technology could support an activity not currently supported. Or it could provide additional support in a different way.

Technology support for TLAs can thus be a substitution, deficit-filling, or enrichment, of traditional course elements. Whether any of these are worthwhile will depend on the specific context. The optimum blend of (in this case) five or more methods will depend on their availability and costs, acceptability to the teacher and students, and their mutual compatibility, which only the teacher in the local context can decide.

This book could have been organised by technical characteristics (e.g. multimedia, Web-based, mobile) or by broad categories of function (e.g. resources, tools, simulations, surrogate teachers, and communication media) (see Bostock, 1996, for a discussion of classifications). Instead, it is organised by TLAs in the hope that this is more helpful to teachers thinking about their teaching. However, lists of appropriate TLAs will be different for different disciplines and topics, and the total list would be very long. Even a general scheme of common TLAs would have about 30 (see Oliver and Conole, 1998). This book aggregates TLAs into five categories, based on the ways a student can engage with the teacher, the subject, or fellow students. The modes of student engagement have been used to structure face-to-face teaching (Bostock, Hulme and Davys, 2006) but they seem to work for online activities, too (Figure 2). Most courses should have TLAs in each of the five modes. Modes 1 and 2 are perhaps a continuum of types of presentations, onsite and online, with a similar relationship between teacher and student. Nonetheless, it seems worthwhile distinguishing them, if only to be able to compare their potential benefits and problems.

These five broad categories of TLAs do not have a simple, one-to-one fit with teaching methods or with technologies; a TLA category like transmission-reception (mode 1) can involve a teacher, a book or an online document. Rather, there are multiple methods that could support each mode in some circumstances. Conversely, some technologies can serve different modes of engagement when supporting different activities. For example, presentation software (e.g. PowerPoint) can be used in simple and enhanced transmissions, face-to-face

Figure 1 An imaginary course

Student activity	Example – traditional methods	Example – technology-based methods
Information acquisition	Reading a set book, lectures	Web documents
Skills practice	Problem sheets in classes	Computer simulations
Discussion	Tutorials	Asynchronous text discussions
Discovery	A field trip	Finding and evaluating Web resources
Assessment	Essay questions in a closed exam	Computer-based assessment using multiple choice

or as an online resource (lectures, files). Communication technologies (e.g. e-mail) are often useful for both student-student and student-teacher interaction. Despite these complications (in themselves interesting), it seems worthwhile using a classification based on TLAs.

There is still a broad distinction between onsite (offline) technologies - those supporting teaching and learning in face-to-face (F2F) situations or using technology not requiring network communication - and online technologies - those using the computer network to support student learning, whether individually, with other students or with a teacher. Figure 2 describes examples of the technologies supporting the modes of engagement, both for onsite and online environments. In some cases, software might be accessed either on a stand-alone computer or on a Web server accessed through a browser such as Internet Explorer. Because the Web typically allows access from any browser, problems of varying software, hardware or operating systems are avoided. It is thus a convenient way of providing access to software for an individual, without using other network features, instead of, for example, using a CD-ROM - compact disc read-only memory. In such cases, the technology is treated as onsite in its functionality even though it is used over a network. In other words, the online/onsite distinction is one of learning activities rather than technology.

This framework of ten TLAs (five modes, online and onsite) is used to structure this book; the chapters and sections are given in the table. In places, the onsite/online options are similar and dealt with in one section to avoid duplication. The integration of onsite and online environments is considered in chapter 7.5.

Figure 2 The organiser for the book
(with chapters and sections)

Mode of student engagement (type of TLA)	A. Examples of traditional TLAs	B. Examples of onsite technology supporting TLAs	C. Examples of online technology supporting TLAs
1 **Simple presentation** (transmission/reception)	Students listen and write notes in a didactic lecture, or read a textbook	Microphone, chalk, simple PowerPoint (2.1)	Shovelware (4.1)
2 **Multimedia presentation** (transmission/reception)	Students watch images, videos, demonstrations, debates, discussion panels	PowerPoint, OHP, digital projector with DVD, VCR, interactive whiteboard (2.2, 2.3, 2.4), handouts (2.5)	Image, video, and audio resource files; video and audio streaming; podcasts, multimedia simulations (4.2)
3 **Individual student activity** (interact with content)	Students answer, question, reflect, use a paper Personal Development Portfolio, self assessments, simulations, games, case studies	Gapped handouts (2.5), word processor (3.1), simulations (3.1), writing self assessment documents	Using Web sites, Google, online tutorials and simulations. Writing and self assessment in e-portfolios, blogs (4.3, 4.4)
4 **Student-student interactivity** (interact with peers)	Students engage in discussion, problem-based learning, team projects, fishbowls, role play, peer assessment	Groupware (3.2), Interactive Whiteboard (2.2), Peer assessment of presentations (3.5)	Online discussion or collaboration in discussion boards, wikis, role plays, e-mail, peer assessment, synchronous text chat (6)
5 **Student-teacher interactivity** (interact with teacher)	Students engage in tutorials supervision, mentoring, apprenticeship, internship, formative teacher assessment and student evaluation of courses	Personal response systems in interactive lectures (3.3), computer tutorials (3.1), onsite assessment aids for teachers (3.4)	See C4 above plus Frequently Asked Questions, online assessments, ballots (5)
Or integrated as		Multimedia console (2.2)	Virtual learning environment (7)

1.4 Information Technology skills

Will students have the ICT (Information and Communication Technology) skills you expect of them? In the UK, students' familiarity with computers increases every year due to exposure at school, home and work. There is a UK national framework for ICT skills. The UK Government promotes 'key skills' including ICT (http://www.dfes.gov.uk/keyskills/) and the Qualifications and Curriculum Authority (http://www.qca.org.uk/6507.html) defines four levels of ICT skills in detail, for schools and colleges. Many of your students may have achieved some of these levels. The International Computer Driving Licence ® (ICDL, http://www.icdlap.com), including the European CDL, is a widely recognised qualification in ICT skills. Some institutions offer it to staff and students. Its seven categories are:

1   Basic concepts

2   Using computers and managing files

3   Word processors

4   Spreadsheets

5   Databases

6   Presentations

7   The Internet and e-mail.

In response to the DfES skills agenda, many universities have developed their own descriptions of graduate student learning outcomes in generic skills (sometimes called employability skills) including ICT skills. The following are the intended 'employability' skills in ICT for bachelor degrees at my university. Graduates will be able to:

1   Create, open, delete, rename, back up and store files and check them for viruses

2   Access information from a number of electronic sources including library catalogues, databases and the World Wide Web and use online search facilities

3   Use e-mail to send and receive messages and files

4   Produce electronic documents including essays, reports, dissertations and presentation slides in appropriate formats

5   Input data, perform basic calculations and create appropriate charts using statistical or spreadsheet software.

As well as being useful for later employability, these are essential skills for learning on many programmes. Programmes should have a framework, such as a tabular map, of the ICT skills (and other generic skills) that are required, taught, practised, or assessed (formatively or summatively) in each course (module). If no such framework exists for your course(s), you still need to make clear to students the ICT skills involved, and (if you are not going to teach them) how they can develop them outside the course if they need to, for example using resources or workshops from your institution's information services or learning support unit. Some groups of students, such as older students, international students, and those from less affluent backgrounds, may be unfamiliar or even hostile to ICT; they may need more support. All students need to be told why you are using any chosen technology.

These are generic ICT skills but using some of the technologies discussed in this book, in the context of learning activities, will require more specific skills, such as team-working using an online discussion board or an interactive whiteboard. Students will need training in these technologies, albeit brief, and discussion about their effective use. A good tactic is to admit that you are a novice yourself and that you will all be learning together how to use the chosen technology for the purposes of the course. Ask if any students are familiar with it; they can teach others. We cannot assume that everyone already has the necessary skills and so leave some students struggling or disheartened.

Technical IT skills are just a part of a broader 'information literacy', where they overlap with library skills and have a number of aspects concerning information sources, processes, control, and construction (Oliver and Smith, 2005). Even if they have the technical skills, students need to be taught information skills from the perspective of their programme.

What ICT skills will you need? Using the ICDL list above, you will need to understand basic concepts, files and operating systems (like MS Windows), word processing, presentation, and use of the Internet (1, 2, 3, 6, 7). This is similar to the list of employability skills above except that you will probably not need skills with databases or spreadsheets unless they are important in your discipline, in which case you should already have them. In 1999, I wrote a list of ICT skills outcomes for a teacher induction course. New teachers should be able to:

1   Use a Windows environment, including multiple applications and the clipboard

2   Use a word processor

3   Use personal e-mail to send messages and attachments to individual staff, students and groups

4   Join, use and leave an e-mail list such as those maintained at http://www.mailbase.ac.uk

5   Use a Web browser and keep a list of favourites/bookmarks

6   Use the Internet to find and evaluate relevant resources

7   Participate appropriately in (and lead) online discussions

8   Create a home Web page and a simple Web document for student use, including links to local and global documents

9   Evaluate computer-based learning resources in their own discipline with a view to integrating them into their own teaching.

In any course or module you are teaching, you obviously need the ICT skills expected of, or being learnt by, the students.

Generic ICT skills, such as those above, are not pedagogical, teaching skills. However, the two sets of skills overlap in the uses of technology in teaching and learning. That is the subject of this book, and of various staff development frameworks. In Further Education, the FERL Practitioner's Programme contains statements of many detailed competencies in ICT as a teacher (http://ferl.becta.org.uk/display.cfm?page=403). In Higher Education that approach is unpopular. Alongside short training courses and materials on technical skills, such as those provided by Netskills (http://www.netskills.ac.uk/), longer courses stress the educational issues in using ICT. The staff development outcomes developed by the EFFECTS project, from 1998 to 2001, were adopted by SEDA as one of its Professional Development Framework awards (http://www.seda.ac.uk/pdf/). The Embedding Learning Technologies award (ELT) is the basis of staff development programmes in a number of universities (Bostock, 2005b). Such ELT programmes expect staff to:

1   Conduct a review of IT in learning and teaching and show an understanding of the underlying educational processes

2   Analyse opportunities and constraints in using IT and selected IT appropriate to the learning situation

3   Design a learning resource, programme or activity to integrate appropriate IT

4   Implement a developed strategy

5   Evaluate the impact of the intervention

6   Disseminate and embed the findings of the evaluation.

This is a scholarly approach based on action research into the professional practice involving the design, implementation and evaluation of an innovation in teaching or the support of learning. (At Keele University, I have taught such a programme annually since 2001.) Technical ICT skills are not award outcomes but some programmes will provide these alongside, and the award outcomes require staff to plan and reflect on their professional development, including technical skills.

Whether or not you undertake such a programme later, to have the ICT and pedagogical skills you need, plan your own development systematically. Using the steps built into all programmes recognised by SEDA's Professional Development Framework awards:

1   Identify your directions and priorities for professional development

2   Plan how to achieve that development; make a timetable

3   Undertake appropriate development activities (using a range of methods including courses, guides, books, helpdesks, mentors)

4   Then review your development and how it helps your practice, and start again.

1.5 Securing your information

As you make greater use of computer-based technology, you will become more dependent on it. Your electronic documents will become invaluable; you need a routine to minimise the risks of loss that, while not being too onerous, you are confident could provide you with up-to-date copies of everything should you need them. When working on a document, save it frequently - it is usually a single key-press (ctrl-s) - in case of a power cut or disk crash. A working (master) copy on your PC's fixed (or 'hard') disk and a second (backup) copy of everything is a minimum. However, you or the computer can make a mistake *during* the copying process so that only when it is too late do you discover that you do not have a good second copy. And what if the building burns down? You should keep a third copy in another location. You can also make long-term archives of work you do not expect to use again, so that you are not repeatedly backing it up with your current data.

Computers fail, and are stolen, without warning. Imagine yours failed now - how much work would you lose? How long would it take to replace? What is the salary cost of that time? (And the stress!) Storage media such as CD-ROMs, USB memory sticks, and hard disks are cheap in comparison. If you have access to a network drive of sufficient capacity, use that for your first backup; an external hard disk that plugs into a PC's USB (universal serial bus) port, or a CD-ROM disc can be another. Temporary, working copies of files can also be held on a USB memory stick or a PDA (personal digital assistant) but these are easy to lose.

For example, I make a backup of new or modified data files (an incremental backup) onto an external hard disk at the end of every day, or even when I leave the office. It takes a single mouse click. The copying process resets 'the archive bit' on those files so they will not be re-copied unless they are modified again; this makes the incremental backup process quick (less than a minute). I make a backup of all data files weekly at home, on another external hard disk. (This does not re-set the archive bit, otherwise the office copies get out of synchrony.) As I occasionally reorganise the folder structure, I start a new full copy in the office every month and add my daily incremental backups to it.

I make read-only archives on CD-ROM at the end of every year. With at least three copies of everything, losing a computer is a nuisance but not a crisis. It happened to me last in 2004 but I was up-and-running on an old laptop within an hour, with a copy of everything from the previous day. Don't drive your computer without a safety belt and airbags!

To make both working with your files, and backing them up, simpler and safer, organise them in a hierarchy of folders according to their use (for each course, lecture, research project, etc.). Keep all your data folders in one master folder (*My Documents* in MS Windows), and then back up this folder in your own routine. Keep your e-mail and your Web addresses where they also get backed-up (or make other arrangements to secure them). Then, pretend to lose your computer (don't erase the working copy!) and test if you can restore all your data onto another computer. If everything is there, you can sleep easy. To make the copies you could use your operating system's backup and restore facility. However, with MS Windows Backup you must use Windows Restore to retrieve the files, and a different version of Windows might have difficulty restoring (it has happened!). So, I make normal copies of files, but I use a batch file containing the XCOPY command, run by a single click on an icon. Ask your local technician if you need help setting up a backup process.

You must use a virus checker (e.g. Norton AntiVirus) and keep it up to date, otherwise you are taking a big risk with your data and equipment. Worse, if you pass on a virus in the files or e-mails you give to students, your reputation will plummet. If you use the Internet much, you should use a firewall (there is one in Windows XP). It is also worth considering using a 'malware' scanner (e.g. XoftSpy) to get rid of advertising and snooping software that you will pick up unknowingly. You need to configure your browser for blocking pop-ups, for security and privacy (see *Tools, Internet Options* in Internet Explorer).

1.6 Further reading

On IT skills

More detail of Embedding Learning Technologies is at the ELT Web site, http://www.elt.ac.uk/

The Big Blue project surveyed Information Skills Training for students in Post-16 Education. The project *'will assist in ensuring a coherent approach to the development of an information literate student population in the UK'* (http://www.leeds.ac.uk/bigblue/toolkitpost16.html).

Big Blue Connect was *'a Joint Information Systems Committee (JISC) funded project to investigate the information skills sets of staff working in the Higher and Further Education sectors'* (http://www.library.mmu.ac.uk/bbconnect/index.html).

JISC has recently (August 2005) completed a project on *Staff Information Skills Set,* http://www.jisc.ac.uk/project_siss.html, which includes a model for professional development in information handling (not necessarily IT) skills.

Littlejohn, A. H. and Stefani, L. A. J. (1999) 'Effective use of communication and information technology: bridging the skills gap', *ALT-J,* 7 (2): 66-76.

On blended learning

A Guide for Teachers - e-Learning Series No.3, http://www.heacademy.ac.uk/resources.asp?process=full _record&section=generic&id=323

Effective Practice with e-Learning, from the UK JISC, is a *'a good practice guide to designing learning aimed at practitioners in further and higher education',* http://www.elearning.ac.uk/effprac/

A recent Centre for Excellence in Teaching and Learning is the University of Hertfordshire's Blended Learning Unit, http://perseus.herts.ac.uk/uhinfo/info/blu/

For Further Education, see ICT and e-learning in Further Education, http://www.becta.org.uk/research/research.cfm? section=1&id=3437

For an example of university e-learning in the US, the March 2002 issue of *Teaching with Technology,* 8 (6), is a special edition on 'hybrid courses', http://www.uwsa.edu/ttt/browse/hybrid.html

Some typical elements of online courses were described by Carr-Chellman, A. and Duchastel, P. (2000) 'The ideal online course', *British Journal of Educational Technology,* 31 (3): 229-241.

(All Web sites accessed on 25 November 2005)

Chapter 2 Face-to-face presentations

This chapter discusses the technologies supporting onsite (face-to-face) presentations and multimedia presentations (mostly cells B1, B2, and B6 in the Organiser).

2.1 Lectures

What's the use of lectures? (Bligh, 1998).

Lectures are still a common feature of many university courses. It was the default teaching method – many teachers have contracts as *lecturers*. The literature on such traditional lectures is damning about their effectiveness for student learning (Bligh 1998, Laurillard 2002). Listening and note-taking for any length of time are difficult and often boring. Merely displaying content does not achieve student learning. Students are placed in a passive role that is ineffective for learning. And if teaching as dictation is ineffective for learning, teaching as writing on the board or projecting prepared text with PowerPoint is little better. Copying your spoken or written notes may provide students with a set of notes but, if that is the aim, photocopies or a Web document would do a better job.

However, what happens in a lecture theatre need not be a didactic monologue. Andreson (1990) suggested two strategies: (i) *refinement* of the lecture as theatre, enhancing the presentation skills of the teacher and the technology used, or (ii) *augmentation* of the didactic lecture with student activity, feedback, and dialogue. Within a course, we can do both: less lecturing but better lecturing. In terms of the modes of engagement, this means replacing excessive use of simple presentations (mode 1) with mixtures of all the five modes.

Enhancing a presentation might involve a practical demonstration or a debate between colleagues, with no technology involved. However, you can easily use technology to present images or sound or video. The importance of visual displays of images or text to students will vary between subjects, but it will improve the effectiveness of many presentations, for example, showing images of subject content, helping visualisation of concepts or models, demonstrating a skill, or providing an outline structure for the content. For most people, learning is often helped by seeing as well as listening (Smith, 1997, p.14). Some students have particularly visual learning styles (Riding and Rayner, 1998).

With groups of more than 50 your voice will benefit from a microphone. Even if you can project your voice, a microphone allows a greater range of intonation, and may save you a sore throat. A radio microphone – either clip-on or hand-held – allows you to walk about the room rather than being chained to a lectern – useful for keeping contact with those at the back. You can also use it in question-and-answer sessions by passing it to students but don't forget to switch it off when going to the nearby toilets!

2.2 Visual displays

We live in interesting times, technologically. One hundred years ago, 'learning technology' was a blackboard for the teacher and slates for the students. We are now seeing the replacement of paper and analogue technologies (e.g. videotape) with digital ones (e.g. electronic books and digital video). The technologies available to enhance presentations are a wide range from the traditional to the digitally advanced.

Especially when teaching with unfamiliar equipment, it is wise to have a backup plan. For example, if you take your PowerPoint file on a memory stick, have another way of accessing it if you need to, such as placing it on the Web, or in an e-mail to yourself, or on a CD-ROM. For important occasions you may want to take foils ready to use on an OHP (overhead projector). Ultimately you could teach from the handouts or with a whiteboard or chalkboard. 'Be prepared' is not just for Scouts!

Chalkboards, whiteboards

Talk and chalk is the caricature of traditional lecturing but, if that's all the technology there is, you can still use it well. Thirty years ago when I did my teacher training course, we were trained to write clearly on a chalkboard, and I wished some of the lecturers in my degree course had done that training! Legibility on old boards can be poor so you need to write large, clear text and diagrams for those with poor eyesight or those at the back of the room. (Go there and check for yourself.)

While a few may like being covered in chalk dust, most people and all computers are better without it. So chalkboards are disappearing (except in maths departments), to be replaced by whiteboards. With a good marker pen, these are easier to read. A disadvantage is that the pens need to be 'dry marker' not permanent ink, and, if there is one left by the board, it has probably run out. Take your own. It is an academic sin to use a permanent ink pen, which neither you nor later users of the room can remove.

Another claimed disadvantage is that while the last generations of chalkboards rolled over or slid over each other to give more writing space, whiteboards are usually a single surface. This may be less of a problem to students than to the teacher who must clean the board to create writing space (take a cloth or tissues – the board rubbers are often dirty). Anyway, we may question the effectiveness of a teaching-learning activity that involves so much copying.

Overhead projectors

An overhead projector (OHP) can be a great tool: simple to use, giving a large, bright image of prepared foils or impromptu, hand-written notes. Their disadvantages are few: the lens or illuminated surface can be dirty; they can be cleaned with a tissue. As OHPs are often moved, on trolleys or just carried about, they often need adjusting. If the image is not positioned well on the screen, adjust the angle of the mirror or rotate it (if it will), or move the OHP. The image can be focussed using the adjustment knob on the arm or the OHP body to move the lens up or down (Figure 3). The bulb can be out of alignment, causing an uneven or blue light; there should be an internal focussing mechanism, or the lever to switch to a second bulb may not be fully in place. You can get a bright, horizontal, focussed image before you start. What you cannot do is prevent key-stoning – having the image wider at the top than at the bottom. This is not a problem unless you are projecting very high in a large room, in which case the screen should be inclined forwards to compensate. Most other screens can also be inclined unless they descend from the ceiling.

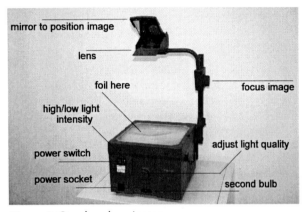

Figure 3 Overhead projector

One risk with an OHP is that the bulb fails while you are using it. Most models have a spare bulb that can be switched into place with a lever at the base of the body – look for it before you start teaching. Switch the projector off before switching bulbs. A cautious person would check that both bulbs work before starting. Replacing the bulb with a new one requires technical help or instruction.

Foils can be prepared by printing them directly from your computer (you need the right sort for your printer) or by photocopying paper copies onto foils. It is a mistake to put an A4 printed sheet, or a page from a book, on an A4 foil: the text projected on the screen will be too small. Text size is usually measured in 'points', with 72 points to the inch. Text on a foil needs to be at least 20 point to be readable (about twice the size of text in most books), and preferably 28 point, depending on the screen size and the room. Foils are A4 but the projected image is square – wider but not as tall. So you cannot use the full height of a foil (in portrait orientation) without having to move it up and down on the OHP, which is a nuisance for you and the students.

In use, it is generally a mistake to try to reveal parts of a slide, line by line, by moving a sheet of paper down it.

It is irritating for the audience and the paper often blows off (the cooling fan seems designed to do that). A better alternative is to place a pen on the acetate to indicate the part you are talking about. Another common mistake is to block the view of the displayed image for some students by standing in the way. This is a particular problem if you are writing on the acetate: you will need to move to one side after writing, so that all students can view the image.

Digital projectors

Digital projectors, sometimes called 'multimedia' projectors, are becoming common as fixtures in teaching rooms, and portable ones are simple to set up and connect to the video (RGB) output of a desktop PC or laptop. Wireless projectors are becoming affordable, so if you have a laptop with a wireless network adapter (wifi) you should, in future, be able to connect wirelessly to the projector – much simpler than fitting a cable between the two. Digital projectors are typically not as bright as OHPs but they are easily focussed (a ring around the lens); the lens should not need cleaning, and they can be adjusted for key-stoning. Their filters need cleaning occasionally but that is not your job (even though your laptop may remind you to do it). With portable projectors, after switching off, they should not be moved until they have cooled themselves by running the fan for a few minutes, otherwise the bulb life is reduced, and they are expensive. The resolution (detail) of the display is not a good as an OHP or 35mm slides but most current projectors have XGA displays (1024 pixels – dots – wide and 768 high). This is good enough for most purposes except, say, detailed photographic images.

The main difference from an OHP is, of course, that all the text and images to be displayed must be on the computer connected to the projector. If the computer is fixed in the room, you must access your information by a network connection or bring it with you on a USB memory stick (recommended) or other storage medium that is readable on that PC. Having all your presentation materials on your computer may sound like a chore but in the long run it is flexible and saves time. If there is no projector available, you could print them on foils for an OHP, or print them as handouts.

Visualisers

A visualiser combines the ability of an OHP to display transparencies, by transmitted light from below, with the ability to display books and papers by reflected light from above. They are becoming common in lecture theatres, displaying through a digital projector. You can display foils if you have them, or original books or papers, or even objects, which you can zoom in on. The comments about using OHPs apply here.

Interactive whiteboards

Interactive whiteboards (IWBs) typically consist of a PC, a digital projector, and a special solid screen that detects the position of a stylus (a 'digital pen') used on it. The board is simultaneously a screen and an input device. There are different IWB technologies: some IWBs are pressure sensitive so you can write with your finger, others are arrays of sensors that are bolted onto the edges of traditional whiteboards, and others detect a special stylus using a grid below a tough white surface. They are really 'digital whiteboards'; how 'interactive' they are depends on how they are used.

Their advantage is flexibility: you can use one simply as a screen to display PowerPoint slides or any other computer image; or you can use the stylus on the IWB (instead of a mouse) to control the computer display; or you can use a graphical computer application, such as the 'flipchart' software shipped with them, to write on the board in 'electronic ink'. More sophisticated uses might include moving graphical objects around the board with the stylus, or having students use the board to create a shared digital record of group work. With an IWB you have the flexibility to display anything from the PC, and use its flipchart software to make ad hoc notes. Anything you create or modify can be saved and later re-used, printed or made available on the Web or in a virtual learning environment (VLE).

Normally, the projector is in front of the board so you need to avoid writing in your own shadow. Obviously, you should not turn to look directly into the projector. Other disadvantages of IWBs include the need for the special stylus, which are too expensive to leave in public rooms, and, if the projector is moved at all, the stylus position must be calibrated to place the screen pointer exactly under the physical stylus. Despite these possible difficulties, with some training and a little practice, they are very flexible teaching tools. Students are increasingly familiar with them as they are popular in UK schools.

Multimedia

Until recently, presenting images, sound or video used analogue technologies like 35mm slides and audio or video tape but they are being replaced by digital CD-ROMs (Compact Disc Read-Only Memory) for audio and DVDs (Digital Versatile Disc) for video. These give better quality and more control over which clips or sections you want to present. Whether from analogue tape or digital disk, playing through a sound system and a digital projector gives more detail and impact than using a television. If you don't have a digital display system in the room, a portable projector and a loudspeaker on the PC, DVD or VCR (video cassette recorder) can still provide a good viewing experience; most PCs will play DVDs and music CDs. It is increasingly easy to create and present computer-integrated multimedia. Modern PCs handle images and audio easily, and digital video with a little effort. Producing multimedia is discussed in section 2.4.

Many teachers find video extremely useful, if suitable content is available (Barford and Weston, 1997). It can

add variety and realism to a presentation or other teaching session. Video is usually used in clips of a few minutes. For students to get the most from a clip, its purpose in the session needs to be explained – what should they be listening or watching for?

(See also sections 2.4, 4.2, and 4.5)

Panels

The computer 'mouse' was invented in the 1960s as a pointing device. Most of us learn to use it but it can be inconvenient when teaching and it is hopeless if we want to write or draw free-hand. In the absence of an interactive whiteboard, we can do this with a special PC screen that is also an input device – you draw on the screen, like a small interactive whiteboard. The panel is a screen that is sensitive to a stylus (digital pen). You can write freehand notes that are displayed through the digital projector, along with any prepared slides or other displays. The panel could be embedded in a lectern or on a cable allowing you to pass it around a table in a smaller room.

Tablet PCs

Tablet PCs are laptops, a portable version of a PC with a panel screen/input device. Some are dedicated to work only in this way, and have no keyboard or mouse, just an interactive tablet/screen. Others are hybrids that allow you to work either with a keyboard and mouse or with a stylus on the screen. The Tablet version of MS Windows XP also has handwriting and voice recognition utilities; such software has improved steadily in recent years (and I used handwriting recognition on a tablet PC to create the first draft of some of this book).

However, the real benefit when teaching is to be able to control the PC with a stylus and to hand-write and hand-annotate when teaching, on presentation slides or an electronic flipchart. If connected wirelessly to a wifi digital projector, a battery-powered tablet PC is a flexible, portable teaching device. You can walk about with it in class, or pass it around the room for others to read or write on, and have the tablet display simultaneously displayed on a large screen.

Pointing devices

During presentations with a large screen it is often useful to point to particular parts of the screen. With an OHP you can place something on the acetate surface but then you have to move back and forth to the projector. With a computer display you can use the mouse to control the pointing device. If this chains you to the lectern or PC, there are portable alternatives. Wireless mice and keyboards can be used from anywhere in the room to control a PC for a PowerPoint presentation, although some have a limited range. There are also wireless 'multimedia presenters' (Figure 4) designed for this purpose – hand-held controllers with buttons for changing slides, controlling the mouse pointer, and so on. They usually also contain a laser

Figure 4 Multimedia presenter

pointer that projects a bright point or arrow onto the screen. In any case, a laser pointer (or 'laser pen') is worth having.

Multimedia Consoles

Increasingly, teaching rooms have consoles or lecterns housing a networked PC, and maybe a VCR, a DVD player, and a visualiser, all connected to a digital projector and loudspeakers (Figure 5). They have an RGB (red-green-blue) socket (and hopefully a cable) for your laptop, and a power socket for it. There may be a wireless mouse and keyboard or a multimedia presenter. If there is a console available in your teaching room, get someone to give you a quick tour of its facilities, then practise with those you will use.

Figure 5 Multimedia console

Video links from a lecture theatre to other rooms or other sites are sometimes installed to allow additional students to take part in the lecture, for example by remotely presenting the audio and video of the lecturer plus the display on the digital projector. If you find yourself using one of these, check what the overflow students can see and hear. Their experience is unlikely to be better than for those with you in the room and may well be worse (Freeman, 1998; Fillion, Limayem and Bouchard, 1999; Knipe and Lee, 2002), especially as the 'lecture' becomes more interactive (see 3.3).

2.3 Presentation software

The increased availability of digital projectors is making presentation software ubiquitous (for convenience, I will refer to MS PowerPoint from now on). There are advantages of using PowerPoint:

1 The structure of slides and lines (bullets) automatically creates a hierarchy of information 'bites' that often helps students organise the information

2 The consistency of layout, fonts, and colours and so on, helps students concentrate on the content, not the design

3 Automatic features such as slide numbering, headers and footers provide orientation information for students

4 You can copy and paste information from other documents like Web pages or word processor documents. It is easy to include digital photographic images, sounds and video in slides

5 The same information can be presented with minimal effort in multiple ways: slide, handout, Web page, outline document

6 The 'Outline' view can be helpful for planning or pasting text

7 The 'Notes' view allows you to keep your own notes attached to slides and print them together

8 The 'Master' views enable you to create and change layouts, and other features of all slides in a presentation, in a single action.

On the other hand, there are pitfalls:

1 The hierarchy of slides and bullets can distort the natural structure of a subject where, say, narrative or debate would be more appropriate

2 The ready-made slide templates or 'themes' are unsuitable for educational purposes; they reduce readability, are distracting and can be printed/ photocopied badly. They have smaller fonts for sub-bullets but the students still need to be able to read that information (change them in the slide 'Master' view)

3 The animated entrance of text is irritating for the audience and makes navigation in an 'on-screen presentation' difficult (e.g. going backwards)

Good design is partly a personal preference but here are some good principles:

1 Avoid textured or photographic backgrounds, bright colours, and fancy font faces: they all reduce readability

2 Black text on a pale coloured background, or white text on a dark colour, gives good contrast for readability

3 Don't put too much text on one slide: a few main points will help students to structure their understanding

4 Numbering the lines on a slide is often more helpful than bullets.

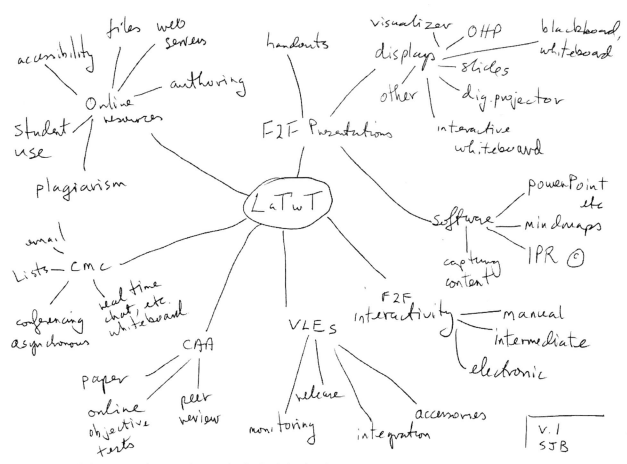

Figure 6 Hand drawn mind map of an early draft of this book

PowerPoint and digital projectors are not necessary for each other: when making a presentation, you can display screens of information from a word processor document, a Web page, or an electronic flipchart; conversely you can use PowerPoint to create foils for an OHP. Nonetheless, there are advantages in using the two together, using an 'on-screen presentation':

1   PowerPoint slides are the right shape (3 by 4) for current projectors (XGA), or they are automatically adapted from a different original shape

2   You can control the display of slides, navigating forwards, backwards and to any other slide, blanking the screen temporarily, and so on

3   From PowerPoint 2002 on, you can add handwritten annotations to slides (in digital 'Ink') to add some spontaneity, although you will need a better pointing device than a mouse, like a tablet or interactive whiteboard, to write anything readable. From the 2003 version on you can then save these annotations as a record; you can thus use blank slides as a digital flipchart

4   You can put hypertext links into slides to show Web sites or other documents

5   Simple animations are also easy, like building a diagram from its components, or labelling parts of a photograph.

Slides should be an aid for presenting information in a clear, organised, engaging, and memorable way. Listening to a presenter slavishly reading the slides of text is as tedious as presentations can be, but this 'Death by PowerPoint' is no better or worse than (intellectual) death by OHP foil or death by dictation. It is not a condemnation of the technology but of the presenter's use of the technology.

Mind maps

Mind maps are diagrams showing the relationships between concepts. They are often a hierarchy rearranged into a concentric diagram. They are valuable as graphical organisers, giving an overview of a subject and showing the relationships between concepts rather than the detail of concepts. Some students take notes as mind maps and will appreciate a map of your course or lecture.

Although hand-drawn mind maps are richer in detail, and better for learning when drawing your own (Buzan, 1993), for most of us drawing one by hand is time-consuming and the product is messy as a course document. Software packages are available. For example, Figure 7 (overleaf) is a mind map of this book drawn with Matchware OpenMind2, which used the chapter and section headings in the MS Word document for the nodes in the map. Figure 6 is a hand drawn mind map of an earlier version, drawn on a Tablet PC with the interactive whiteboard (IWB) flipchart software ActiveStudio.

Figure 7 A mind map of this book

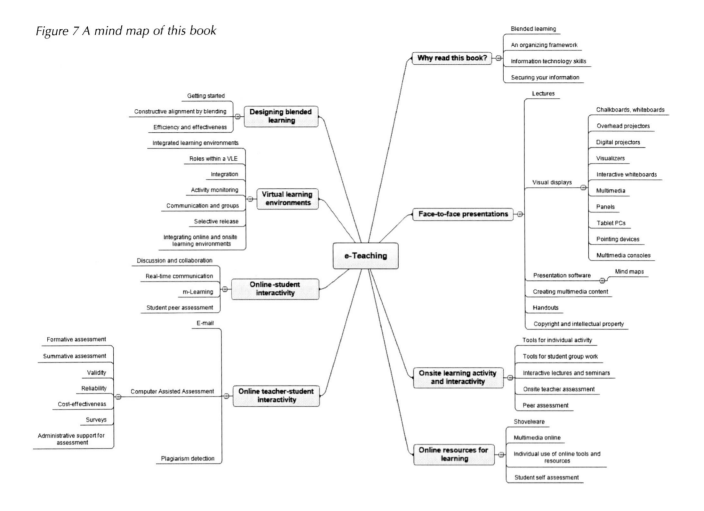

2.4 Creating multimedia content

You probably know how to produce text for a presentation using MS Word or PowerPoint (or alternatives) – if not, consider a training course. However, presenting images, audio or video gives us different problems. In principle, the process is the same as for text:

1 We need an original source

2 We edit it to correct mistakes, improve its appearance, and make it appropriate for use

3 We embed it into the final document that students will see.

With text, the source is our own knowledge, or an existing source we are copying; editing for sense and for appearance can be done in Word or PowerPoint; and it can be embedded in a slide or document, ready for display.

With images, the initial source can be a print or a 35mm slide or a digital image. If you have 35mm slides, you may be able to find teaching rooms with projectors for

them for a while longer, but in the long run it will be easier to have them scanned to digital images and display them digitally. A print can be displayed directly on a visualiser, or photocopied onto acetate for an OHP. If you want to incorporate it into a digital presentation, it can be scanned on a flat bed scanner to produce a digital copy. Modern scanners produce images of greater quality and detail than you can display on a digital projector, or on an ordinary office printer, but good advice is to make this initial digital copy as high quality as you could ever need, so that you never have to scan the print again.

If you are going to create your own images, a digital camera is convenient. You can transfer the images onto your PC, for example, via a USB cable. The image quality will generally be more affected by the quality of the lens and your ability as a photographer than the number of megapixels in the image. Digital projectors (XGA) display less than one megapixel (one million dots). However, it is useful to start editing an image about twice the size of the final one.

Typically, we edit the initial image to improve it visually and also to reduce its file size to what is necessary for the visual quality needed for projection or printing. You need image editing software such as Paint Shop Pro or the photo editor with MS Office. Editing usually involves: cropping the edges to show what is important in the image as large as possible in the final image; adjusting the colour balance, brightness and contrast for clarity; and reducing the image size (in pixels) and the number of colours per pixel (colour depth) so that the file is much smaller. Then it can be imported (rather than pasted) into a Word document or PowerPoint slide, and positioned for final use. In recent versions of Word and PowerPoint it is possible, and easier, to import an original image file and do the editing there, with similar results.

Images are stored in files of different types (different internal structure) with different file 'extensions' (the three or four letters at the right after the dot). Some types of files store some types of images better. All of them 'compress' the data to different degrees, to reduce the file size. The commonest are:

1   .jpeg or .jpg files – good for photographs. You can choose exactly how small you want the file to be by progressively losing detail in the image, but you can halve most files without noticeable effect

2   .gif – good for diagrams or cartoons with few colours

3   .png – a more recent format for either type of image.

If you only want to display the digital images, you do not need to incorporate them into PowerPoint or another type of document; Windows (XP) Explorer or free software such as IrfanView will do that from the original files.

A similar process is needed for developing sound clips. If your original is on audio tape, you may be able to play it directly. To embed it in a digital presentation we go through the same three steps. To capture a digital version, connect a headphones output from an audio player to the microphone input on a PC. If your PC has a 'line in' plug you can connect that to 'line out' from an audio player or amplifier. A built-in accessory like MS Windows Sound Recorder will capture the sound. It will also capture conversation or other live sounds through a microphone directly to your PC. Place the microphone as far from the computer as possible to reduce background noise, and make the recording in a quiet place.

Windows Sound Recorder allows simple editing of digital sound: copying and pasting clips, and increasing the volume of the data in the file. To improve the sound in other ways, such as removing background noise, removing sections, or starting and ending the recording neatly ('top and tail'), you will need better sound editing software, such as Audacity.

As with images, you can save sound in files of different formats and different sizes, providing different sound quality. Windows' native file format for digital audio is .wav; others are used but a good, general purpose, file format with smaller files is MPEG. Whereas, with images, the file size is determined by the image size in pixels and the number of colours per pixel, with audio it is determined by the time length of the clip, the frequency of sampling (e.g. 22 kHz), the bit-depth of the sampling (8 or 16 bits), and whether it is mono or stereo. For many purposes, 'radio quality' (8 bit mono, at 22 kHz) is adequate. This produces 21 Kb of file per second of sound. Improving the quality of the sound creates larger files. If you need 'CD quality' it is easier to play an original CD. The popular MP3 format is a version of MPEG that is CD audio compressed by a factor of ten or more, with some loss of information, but not that can easily be detected by the human ear. AAC (Advanced Audio Coding) and WMA (Microsoft's Windows Media Audio) formats achieve even greater compression with equal or better sound.

Incorporating sound into PowerPoint or Word is simple. Inserting an audio file into a document produces a loudspeaker icon, which plays the sound when it is clicked.

The capture and editing of video are more demanding of hardware, software, and expertise, than for images or sound. If you already have useful content on video tape you are best using a VCR while they are still available. Your institution's educational technology unit may be able to digitise them to DVD; few of us have the expertise, the equipment or the time to do it ourselves. On the other hand, if you wish to make new video clips, a digital video recorder is simple to use. Some digital video recorders will capture video straight to a DVD disc, ready to play. In all cases you can download the video to a PC using, for example, a Firewire or IEEE 1394 cable. MS Windows XP includes simple video editing software (MS Movie Maker) that allows you to create videos by adding titles and transitions between clips. It will save your video in the compressed Windows Media Video (.wmv) format that you can play back in Windows Media Player. Windows Movie Maker can also capture uncompressed sound (.wav in Windows) and store them as compressed .wmv files.

Video clips are very large files. For example, a clip of 12 seconds at 25 frames per second and 320 by 240 pixels (about a quarter of the screen wide) is 34 Megabytes as raw, uncompressed video. It looks grainy if played as a full screen. Stored as .mpg it is 811 Kbytes and as .wmv it is 635 Kbytes. A clip of three minutes of the same quality is over 5 Mb even when compressed as a .wmv file. Longer clips take a long time to edit and process and, later, to load during a presentation. So, while creating short clips from a digital camera is feasible, anything longer is best left to experts with better equipment and software.

2.5 Handouts

Broadly, there are two reasons to give paper handouts to students: providing information (mode 1), and as a basis for learning activity (modes 3, 4 and 5). In a presentation, most students cannot simultaneously listen, watch, understand, and write coherent notes. You may be transmitting more information than they can receive intelligently. You can help students by providing copies of outlines or mind maps, and telling them what you expect them to make notes of (otherwise some will assume little, others will assume everything). You also need to give them copies of detailed information such as quotations and diagrams – copying these by hand is time consuming and prone to error. Providing such information on the Web is an alternative to photocopying, and is a backup for those who do not receive the paper. If handouts are available in advance on the Web, those with disabilities who are slower to make notes can be prepared.

At this point, let's tackle an old chestnut, 'If I put all my handouts on the Web, they won't come to my lectures'. My experience is that giving handouts at the start of lectures or the start of the course does not badly affect attendance, but the first response must be that, if the only function of lectures is the distribution of handouts, we don't need a lecture. There is, possibly, a difference between the value of the lecture as seen by the students and by the teacher. As the teacher, you may believe it is important for students to attend regardless of handouts. If they see the lecture only as a handout collection point, you need to convince them differently. Using the lecture period for enhanced presentations and activities (modes 2, 3, 4, 5) gives them a value to learning beyond the handout. Then, the handout becomes useful, or even necessary, to learning but not sufficient.

This brings us to the second broad function of handouts, to support activity and interactivity. Handouts can, for example, include questions or quizzes that might be marked by a peer or handed to the teacher at the end. They can give information on which to base individual or group activities. If you are using PowerPoint to generate slides, it will generate handout masters easily. The handouts need not be simply a copy of the slides as displayed. They can include questions where the slides displayed include the answers. They can include a diagram where the slides displayed include the labelling. They can include some bulleted headings where the slides include examples. In other words, 'gapped' handouts can be used in conjunction with the slides to support learning activities. You will need to maintain two versions of the presentation file, for the display and for the handouts, or two versions of some slides in a single file, one of which has 'hidden' slides, either for printing or for display, but not both. There are more sophisticated methods of managing different versions but these will suffice.

2.6 Copyright and intellectual property

Intellectual property includes copyright, patents and trade marks. Copyright is a legal issue; someone owns the right to make copies of a work. In the UK (and this section refers to the UK), all original written or recorded material automatically has copyright, but there is no copyright of an idea alone. Copyright on literary, dramatic, artistic, or musical works, Web site materials, computer programmes, and films, lasts for 70 years after the death of the creator. It is 50 years for sound recordings and broadcasts. Within those periods you cannot legally make copies (paper or electronic) for commercial purposes without the permission of the copyright owner (Copyright, Designs and Patents Act 1988). However, you can make single copies for private research or study. How, then, can you give paper copies to students? Universities in the UK pay the Copyright Licensing Agency (CLA) to make copies for educational purposes of small amounts of the materials of which they own a physical copy. Your library or information service will have the details, but they are not likely to cause you a problem with normal practice. If you want to make and use a digital copy of a paper work, permission is more complex (see http://www.cla.co.uk).

Digital information is also subject to copyright: electronic journals, e-books, Web sites, images, software, and so on. Just because you can easily copy it does not give you the legal right to do so. The CLA licence is being extended to cover digital copies. At the time of writing the details are not known so consult your local library or copyright expert. In the case of electronic books and journals, publishers may sell a licence to copy to a university, or give permission to copy for educational purposes, or charge for the right to copy an electronic item. Just because text or images are visible on a Web site does not give anyone the right to copy them. Some Web sites will have statements about allowed use (check the home page). You can always make a link to the page in question on your own Web page, or ask the owners for permission to make a copy for, say, a private Web space for a course. In the case of academic authors, they are usually flattered to be asked and (in my experience) always agree.

Separate from the right to copy is the 'moral' right to be acknowledged as the author of a work, whether paper or electronic. Unlike copyright, this right does have to be asserted and the law offers some protection to authorship. However, you do not, legally, have the right of authorship for work created during employment – your employer does. In practice, universities generally waive that right in some circumstances (e.g. research papers), but arrangements vary so you should check your local arrangement. This issue has sharpened since teachers have been placing their teaching materials on institutional Web sites, whereas paper copies were probably kept individually. As part of scholarly culture

and policies on plagiarism, good practice is to
acknowledge authorship in teaching materials.
HEFCE (2003) publishes a good practice guide
for institutions.

Your institution may have a policy in favour of making
teaching materials public on the Web, or not. Materials
in a VLE space are automatically private. If you have
discretion over public access to your materials, you must
balance the possible disadvantage of other institutions
using them against the benefits to you of the publicity.
My own practice has been to make everything public
except a few complete courses that might be used in
direct competition.

2.7 Further reading

On making presentations
See Race, P. (2001) *The Lecturer's Toolkit*, 2nd edition,
London: Kogan Page, chapter 3, or Race, P. (1999) *2000
Tips for Lecturers*, London: Kogan Page, chapter 2.

The Advanced Presentation Technology Web site,
http://www2.umist.ac.uk/isd/lwt/apt/

Grandgennett, N. and Grandgennett, D. (1997)
'Techniques for improving computer-assisted
presentations', *Innovations in Education and Teaching
International*, 34 (1): 17-23.

Working with Electronic Whiteboards is at the
Becta/FERL Web site,
http://ferl.becta.org.uk/display.cfm?page=864

On handouts
See chapter 4 of Chin, P. (2004) *Using C&IT to support
teaching*, London: RoutledgeFalmer.

The '*Government-backed home of UK Intellectual
Property on the Internet*',
http://www.intellectual-property.gov.uk/

3 Onsite learning activity and interactivity

In this chapter, I discuss a range of technologies to support student individual activities, student group activities, and teacher-student interactivity (Organiser cells B3, B4, B5). I have included onsite assessment in this chapter because it is a major form of teaching-learning activity, whether it is self assessment, peer assessment or teacher assessment. Some of the software applications described run on Web servers and are accessed though a browser rather than on individual PCs, but that is not enough to classify them as online. I have classed as online technologies, in later chapters, only those applications that make use of the network to add functionality for the users.

3.1 Tools for individual activity

Individual learning activities are as varied as the intended learning outcomes they support. Because hardware is fairly standard (networked PCs), we will concentrate on the range of software tools that can support activities. It is useful to distinguish between software tools and digital resources (Conole, 2004). Resources are essentially content, and are generally specific to the discipline, topic and learning outcomes. They can also be used for individual and group learning activities. For example, an electronic document could be evaluated or paraphrased.

Tools, on the other hand, are content-free and allow the learner to carry out a task with their own content. They are usually generic, such as word processors, spreadsheets, or media players. Tools supporting online activity and interactivity will be discussed in chapters 5 and 6. Those that students use individually include:

1 Tools for creating, organising, presenting and disseminating information e.g. MS Word for documents, Composer or FrontPage for Web pages, and PowerPoint for presentations

2 Tools for handling analogue input e.g. Sound Recorder for capturing audio, and (on a Windows Tablet PC) Journal for freehand writing, Sticky Notes for dictation, and Input Panel for voice or handwriting recognition

3 Tools for manipulating and analysing text or numbers e.g. Excel for spreadsheets, SPSS for statistical analysis, NVIVO for textual analysis

4 Tools for storing and managing data e.g. Access as a general-purpose database manager, Reference Manager for references

5 Tools for personal records and reflection e.g. electronic journals, diaries, calendars, notepads, and to-do lists; and support for structured personal development planning e.g. PebblePad

6 Tools for project management e.g. Microsoft Project

7 Tools for visualisation, brainstorming, and mind mapping e.g. MindGenius, Visio.

Students and teachers need support or training to make the best use of tools. For example, most students use a word processor for final copies but many make poor use of its facilities to structure and revise their work, and present it professionally. Take the most widely used tool, MS Word. Good advice would include:

1 Use heading styles to structure the document (and save formatting time). This means formatting documents using standard styles for headings and subheadings ('Heading 1', 'Heading 2'), rather than simply changing the format of individual text blocks

2 Once heading styles are used, the Document Map view can display the heading structure of the document in a panel that can be used for navigation. The Outline view can display the hierarchical structure of a document's sections, without showing the body text. Sections can be moved intact

3 Headers and/or footers can usefully include the current and total page numbers, the author's name and the document title

4 As you redraft a document, keep the old versions in case you change your mind. Save them with numbered file names. (There is a built-in version control with File, Versions, but it can create large files.)

5 Font faces should be simple and few. Bold or italic should be used sparingly and underlining never used. If you prefer students to use a particular layout and appearance, you should provide them with a template with ready-made styles, footers and so on

6 Spelling and grammar checkers, while not always correct, do detect most issues worth considering. The grammar checker can also give readability score, which may prompt some re-writing.

3.2 Tools for student group work

Students work together in formal and informal settings, with and without teachers being present. A significant example is members of a team collaborating towards shared goals. They may use flipcharts or whiteboards for meetings, word processors for minutes and agenda, or project management software for large projects. Any technology will be used only if it helps to achieve their goals, usually by increasing their productivity, rather than giving them an additional task. To be comfortable with a technology they may need support or training.

An example from personal experience involves a particular form of collaborative learning – problem-based learning (Biggs, 2003, 231-240). It has a long history in medicine, where it wholly or partly replaces teaching by lectures. At Keele University, medical students meet in groups of about ten to consider each problem (a medical case) on three occasions. Students perform particular tasks in analysing the text of medical cases and identifying relevant objectives for their own learning. Traditionally, they accomplished these learning activities by writing on large whiteboards but that record was cleaned after each session. In a new building, all the meeting rooms have a networked PC and a ceiling-mounted digital projector. After a year's experimentation, in 2005 all PBL groups are provided with copies of the text of cases on PowerPoint slides that can be displayed and annotated on a large screen during the PBL sessions, either with a wireless keyboard and mouse, or an IWB where the room has one. With PowerPoint 2003 they can use blank slides as digital flipcharts. Using custom-built software, these files are automatically downloaded from, and uploaded to, a Web space that is private to each group. Web access to them is global, with a group password, but the files can only be edited in the PBL meeting rooms. In this way, each group can collectively create shared notes on each case, that are accessible to them individually afterwards. In this example, the use of technology (i) saves time in the PBL sessions by supporting annotation rather than re-writing of parts of the cases, and (ii) allows each group to create shared medical notes related to assessment, including Web sources and captured content (Bostock *et al.*, 2005).

3.3 Interactive lectures and seminars

'Interactive lectures' means lectures with periods of student activities (modes of engagement 3, 4 and 5). Various learning activities by individuals and small groups have been recommended for lectures (Gedalof, 1998; Smith, 1997; Davies, 2000). Examples of these individual activities and group interactivities (modes 3 and 4) include:

1   Annotating from the screen a diagram on a handout

2   A one-minute break in the middle, to stretch and to collect thoughts

3   Comparing notes with those of the person next to them

4   A quiz marked, possibly marked in pairs

5   'Buzz groups' – giving small groups a small task such as a question or problem.

Many such activities do not need technology. They sustain concentration and support learning more than merely listening and watching. However, a problem arises when the teacher wants to collate the results of these individual or small group activities, or interact with the whole group, and here technology can help.

As student numbers in a group increase, feedback between the teacher and individual students becomes increasingly difficult. Traditional ways of interacting with groups include asking for a show of hands, asking for answers to a question, and inviting questions. We can select students, or ask for volunteers, but both of these have problems. We cannot quickly get a census or a representative sample of student understanding or views. So we cannot give instant feedback on them. We can

ask for answers on paper and comment on them in the next session, but the delay in feedback reduces its value. Instant, two-way feedback between a teacher and a large group (mode 5) requires some technology, generically termed a personal response system (PRS). This allows or requires a response from all students, who then get instant feedback from the teacher. At the same time, voting gives information about the students' progress or views, so that the teacher can immediately adapt the teaching to respond to their current needs. By polling all students, a PRS avoids the sampling problems of volunteering and requires participation from all students, which may maintain their attention.

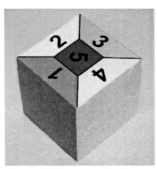

Figure 8 CommuniCube

Before considering electronic voting devices, there are possible 'intermediate technologies'. Coloured cards and similar devices have been used occasionally but, in 2004, I designed a coloured cube, the CommuniCube that allows answers to multiple choice questions with up to five options (http://www.communicubes.com). Each student uses a 10cm cube that has five faces with different colours and the sixth face with a number key (Figure 8). Students select their answer by rotating the cube so they can read the number on the key; they don't think about colours. The teacher sees the different colours, and counts or estimates them. Initial reactions from students over the first year were overwhelmingly positive (Bostock, Hulme and Davys, 2006). This is consistent with research on electronic systems that shows such 'interactive lectures' to be very popular with students (e.g. Boyle and Nicol, 2003).

Electronic voting devices (PRS) are growing in popularity: in the US over a million handsets were sold in 2004 (Phillips, 2005). Each student has a handset with a unique electronic identity (Figure 9) and a number of buttons. One or more detectors in the room are connected to a computer that collects the signals from the handsets. The computer collates the votes and displays the result on a digital projector as a bar chart or pie chart (Figure 10). There are different types of PRS available.

The communication technology between the handsets and the detector is either radio waves or infra-red radiation. Radio detection seems to be faster and, as it is not directional, the handsets do not have to be pointed at the detector, which is a source of error with infra-red handsets.

The software used to display and store the voting data can preserve the anonymity of voting. Alternatively the teacher could store the identity of voters if they always use the same, numbered handsets. The voting pattern

Figure 9 Examples of voting handsets

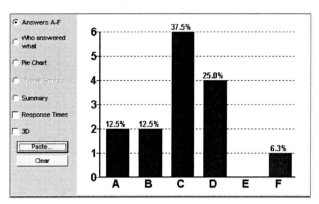

Figure 10 Display of voting result

of individuals may be interesting to the teacher, but the lack of anonymity may change student behaviour. Students can abstain (although they cannot avoid voting with a CommuniCube).

The software allows questions to be asked ad hoc, without displaying them on the screen; or questions can be displayed in PowerPoint slides with the voting software running 'on top'; or a question bank could be prepared in advance and used during the session.

According to Draper and Brown (2004), the uses for a PRS include:

1   Assessment, formative or summative

2   Diagnostic, to influence the content of the lecture

3   Evaluation of the lectures or course by the students (although free-text entries are not possible in most systems)

4   Peer assessment of a student presentation

5   Building mutual awareness in the student body (e.g. age, experience)

6   Responses to human experiments (e.g. in psychology).

Interactivity with a teacher, supported by a PRS, has the advantage of instant feedback between a teacher and a group. By mixing this with other modes of engagement, a variety of student learning activities can be combined, and the benefits of other modes can be enhanced. Perhaps generic patterns of interactive lectures can be developed. A simple pattern, *concept checking*, would be several cycles of a short presentation on a concept (mode 1) ending with a multiple choice test (mode 5). Depending on the result, the next concept is delivered or the current one is further explained and re-tested. A more interesting pattern would be the presentation on a concept (1), a demonstration of its application (2), an individual problem to solve (3), buzz group discussions on the problem answers (4), and a vote on the outcomes of those discussions (5). All the modes have their uses in learning, so a greater variety of modes is likely to be more effective. The detailed design of the student engagement (the content of a presentation, demonstration, problem, discussion, or vote) will

depend upon the subject and the intended learning outcomes for the session.

There are some possible enhancements in the use of PowerPoint where a PRS is being used. Instead of a presentation being a linear sequence of slides, it could be a collection of small sections, some of which are selected on the spot by the teacher depending on the voting pattern. Alternatively, it could have a branching structure, with the pathway determined by the answers, or the preferences, of the audience. Hyperlinks on slides linking to other slides allow easy navigation in an on-screen presentation (Figure 11).

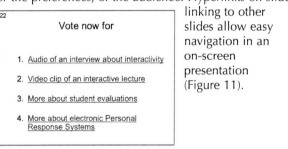

Figure 11 Example PowerPoint screen with hyperlinks

3.4 Onsite teacher assessment

A major form of student interactivity with a teacher is assessment. Without attempting to summarise this vast and important subject, assessment can be before, during and after learning; for diagnosis, for formative feedback on student performance, or for summative grading. Generally, we spend too little time on formative, and too much on summative, assessment (Knight, 2002). Formative assessment, feedback on performance, is essential to learning (and the other two should also have some formative value) but it needs to be timely and informative of how to improve performance. Because of the staff time involved, students often receive less formative feedback than they could use. Can technology help?

Online computer-based assessment is discussed in chapters 5 and 6. This section discusses onsite assessment aids for teachers. Traditionally, the whole assessment process has been paper-based: assignment requirements are provided, coursework is submitted, teachers literally mark the paper with comments and a grade, and the grade is entered on a paper table or 'grade book'. With larger student numbers, some automation can help. Recording and manipulating grades can be done with a custom spreadsheet (e.g. in Excel) or a specialist grade book application (e.g. Turnitin). VLEs come with a grade book that integrates with their other assessment functions. Software can support the writing of feedback comments and printing individualised feedback sheets for students, saving time when giving feedback systematically to large cohorts.

If students submit electronic copies of work, whether online or on disk, you can mark and return their electronic documents in several ways. For example, in MS Word, you can insert footnotes or endnotes into the text with your typed comments. This is the simplest for students to read. Another option is to insert a comment [SJB1] that highlights the relevant text. The comment appears in a balloon on the screen when the mouse pointer hovers over it. If you have a Tablet PC or another device for making handwritten annotations, you can handwrite comments on the electronic document. For these options, *View Markup* must be switched on to see them. To print them, first select *Show* on the reviewing toolbar, then select *Reviewers* and select just the reviewers whose comments are to show (such as the teacher's). When printing, *Print What* in the Print menu should have *Document showing markup* selected.

Specialist software can provide similar facilities. For example, Turnitin's Grademark allows on-screen markup, including inserting typed comments, reference to standard rubrics, and insertion of standard comments for common errors. Whether you can comfortably mark on the screen is an individual preference but larger, clearer screens make it increasingly easy, and I find a Tablet PC is good for hand-annotating most documents.

3.5 Peer assessment

> 'The educational benefits of encouraging students to take responsibility for all aspects of their learning are well rehearsed and many researchers have found that devolving some responsibility to students by involving them in self and peer assessment is an excellent way of enhancing the learning process.' (Falchikov, 2003, p.107)

The practice of scholarship and research is dependent on peer review or assessment, often anonymous. So we could expect that peer (and self) assessment would feature prominently in higher education, at least for diagnostic and formative purposes. Yet assessment is still largely performed by teachers on students.

Technology can be involved in some forms of face-to-face student peer assessment. Oral communication skills are valued in higher education and student presentations are a common way of assessing them. They need an audience and a student audience can take part in their assessment. Students are in a good position to judge the effectiveness of a presentation if it is aimed at an audience such as themselves. Clarity is needed in the assessment criteria (see Wisker, 2004 and Smith, 2004). The use of technology, such as PowerPoint, an OHP, a digital projector, or a handout, should only feature in assessment criteria in so far as it supports the appropriate presentation of information. The audience can each complete a single-sided marking sheet, putting comments and grades against the criteria. These can then be collated by the teacher before being returned to the speaker. Alternatively, a PRS could be used but this might be unnecessarily intimidating. Poster demonstrations are another assessment method where technology and design elements need to be distinguished from content. Again, presentation technology is a vehicle for communicating subject knowledge.

As with all peer assessment, the act of assessing simultaneously provides feedback to the author and practice for the assessor in the use of assessment criteria that may help them with self assessment and improving their own work. (Online support for peer assessment is discussed in section 6.4; student self assessment is discussed in section 4.4.)

3.6 Further reading

Details of the e-learning pedagogy programme and the associated papers and reviews are available from the JISC Web site, http://www.jisc.ac.uk/elearning_pedagogy.html

On lectures
Davies, P. (2003) *Practical Ideas for Enhancing Lectures*, SEDA Special 13.

Gedalof, A. J. (1998) *Teaching large classes*, Green Guide 1, Halifax, Canada: STLHE.

Smith, B. (1997) *Lecturing to large groups*, SEDA Special 1, Birmingham UK: SEDA.

Steve Draper, *Interactive lectures interest group Web*, http://www.psy.gla.ac.uk/~steve/ilig/main.html

Further links on interactivity with large groups are at http://www.keele.ac.uk/depts/aa/landt/links/large_groups.htm

There is a list of gradebook software at http://www.educational-software-directory.net/teacher's/gradebook.html and some free to download at http://www.teach-nology.com/downloads/grading/

Problem-based learning: Special Issue: Challenges of Problem-based learning, issue 2, volume 41, *Innovations in Education and Teaching International*.

4 Online resources for learning

This chapter discusses the use of online resources for individual learning and activity (Organiser cells C1, C2, C3).

Twenty years ago personal computers were isolated. A few of us connected personal computers to larger ones, using a local network or the analogue telephone network, allowing us to collect files, send e-mail, or have online text 'discussions' that were stored in software (bulletin boards) on a central computer. It was tediously slow and you needed technical knowledge. An 'internet' is any network of smaller, local networks. *The* Internet is the one invented in the USA in 1969 that has displaced all others. It has become the global super-network for all sorts of computer-based devices, from Webcams to mobile phones. It had little impact on teaching until the mid 1990s but most of us now find it essential to our work.

We should distinguish the Internet from services based on it, like e-mail and the World Wide Web. The Internet is a medium for sending data that can be the text of an e-mail or the pictures or sounds on a Web page. Services like e-mail and the Web use their own protocols, or rules, to send data across the Internet to be interpreted by software 'clients', like Outlook for e-mail and Mozilla for Web pages, so that we users can see or hear the information they contain.

4.1 Shovelware

Making your teaching documents available online is but one of many uses of the Internet. Shovelware is a disapproving term for simply dumping your teaching documents on the Web in the expectation that it improves student learning; it is usually helpful but never sufficient for learning. As the method of providing information, it can release time from lecturing that can be used to support learning more fruitfully (Anderson, 1997). Let's not be supercilious about providing online access to our information: students need it. In the past, accessing information could waste a lot of time. (In my student days, in the 1970s, information was hard to get. We traveled to libraries to use reference books, and waited for books to be returned by other students.) Before the World Wide Web, information was generally given to students either verbally or on paper. This was inflexible in various ways. The Web provided a technical standard so that anyone with a PC connected to the Internet could access the files on a Web server (Figure 12). Now all that is needed to access a document or file is its address (the Uniform Resource Locator that specifies the server name and the file on it) or a hypertext link to it. Information on the Web is generally available from anywhere at any time: thirty years ago that would have been a miracle. Furthermore, the ease with which Web pages can be created allows teachers or support staff to make collections of linked information (webs) available to students.

Figure 12 The World Wide Web is a client-server information system
(reproduced with permission from Netskills materials at http://www.netskills.ac.uk)

The Web started in 1989 as a simple way of accessing documents from servers in a local network. It has become the global publishing medium: flexible, cheap, and multimedia. Initially, the Web consisted of pages of text embedded with a simple code, hypertext markup language (HTML), enough to format it and provide links to other documents (creating hypertext). Then things became more complex. The client software for Web pages (browsers) became graphical (e.g. Internet Explorer). HTML became more complex with facilities like JavaScript for animation and greater interactivity. Other types of files can be linked from Web pages, such as documents in MS Word or Adobe Acrobat formats, and they will display on the screen if the PC has the necessary software. Animations and multimedia can be embedded in Macromedia Flash files, which are designed to load quickly.

Once students have sufficient access to networked PCs, all the information previously delivered verbally or on paper could be provided through the Web. Shovelware is a start, but merely dumping large amounts of reading material on the Web will not of itself encourage active learning (Meek *et al.*, 1998). That is like handing students a reading list, pointing to the library, and telling them to get on with it. Students need a reading list and a library but that is not the end of teaching (it is only engagement mode 1). Courses should be designed as a blend of teaching-learning activities, using various teaching media and methods. Speech, paper and electronic documents all have their affordances and constraints:

1 Speech in face-to-face meetings is flexible, responsive to students in real time, and it can convey enthusiasm and authority. With large student numbers, it is a cheap use of staff time, assuming the rooms are available. However, it is of limited use for students to gain deep understanding or for providing them with detailed information (Bligh, 1998)

2 Paper is usually easier for reading and annotating than a PC screen. Students like to have paper notes for revision. Handouts can be prompts for learning activities. However, the cost of photocopies, while not large in the overall scheme, can be keenly felt in local

budgets, and they take time to produce. Using a 'set book' transfers the cost to the student but, in the UK, university teachers generally write their own courses

3 Electronic documents are accessible through the Web. Once the computers and network are in place, putting existing documents on a Web server can be very simple, and creating a Web site for a course is not difficult. Then, students can access documents from PC labs on campus, student halls (increasingly networked), home, work, or public libraries, and at any time – peak use is late at night. There are associated costs: the more necessary online documents are, the more students (or their parents) need to buy their own PC and printer, paper and ink. Students need technical support, from the university, or retailers, or parents (I speak from experience!). Teachers have a responsibility to minimise the problems and costs by making their documents easy to access, read, and print.

If you have access to a Web site where you can place course materials (on an ordinary Web server or a virtual learning environment), and this can be a partial or complete replacement for lectures as information provision (Saunders and Klemming, 2003), there are advantages you may not have foreseen. Firstly, it is an online 'home' for the course. Students will know the one place where they can find course documents if they lose paper copies (not all students are well-organised). Secondly, courses do not run on rails, unexpected problems and opportunities arise, and while an e-mail from you should get your students' attention within a few days, a Web site allows you to easily provide permanent copies of new information. Thirdly, it will form an archive for you when planning the course next year, and for students doing 're-sits'.

Since 2002, we have a legal obligation in the UK to make online and print information accessible to students with disabilities (Bostock, 2002). This is not so difficult: the idea of 'design-for-all' is that simple, well-organised Web sites with clear, well-structured documents are easier for everyone to use including those using special equipment to see or hear our documents. Don't be tempted to 'jazz up' a page with arbitrary graphics or animations; they may be an irritation or a puzzle to those who cannot see them, either because their PC cannot display them or because they have a visual impairment.

By far the commonest declared student disability is dyslexia. The following will be helpful to them and to all students:

1 Use a simple, sans-serif font (e.g. Arial, Verdana or Helvetica, or possibly Comic Sans or Lexia)

2 Have a clear structure with consistent heading styles (H1, H2, H3 in HTML)

3 Write in simple words and short sentences as far as possible – try the readability tool in your word

processor (Word has one as part of the spelling and grammar-checking options)

4 Have good contrast between the text and a plain background (e.g. black text on pale blue, green or yellow)

5 Provide more, shorter documents rather than fewer, longer ones

6 Make the visible hyperlinks to another document (what a student would click) descriptive of that document rather than 'click here'.

If there is a document that you want to preserve the format of, you could consider Acrobat PDF format but students' PCs must then have the free Acrobat Reader. Again, you must give them a live link to download it (see 4.4). There have been accessibility problems with PDF files for students with visual disabilities so check that they can access them or provide the information in a generic format like RTF or HTML.

We have considered some issues with online files. Nonetheless, providing information online, in advance, is the single most helpful aid to a student with a disability. He or she should have developed ways of working with electronic documents; if not, send them to student support services for advice. Even so, you should make the offer to students that, if they do have problems with your paper or Web materials, you can provide the information in an alternative format, such as a large print handout, or a disk of documents. If you have the electronic originals it will be easy to do.

4.2 Multimedia online

Why would you want to provide anything online other than text? There are two sorts of reasons: as part of content or as part of the user interface. In some subjects, images or sounds are essential content. A picture or a sound may be worth a thousand words, or none. Even if a description or a transcript is adequate, pictures or sounds can add realism. Animations and video can help students to visualise a process in time or in three dimensions, illustrate how something moves, or add realism and context to an example, especially where human behaviour is involved. Multimedia content can be motivating for students, *showing* them the world instead of talking about it. For example, London Metropolitan University has a demonstration site of professionally produced multimedia at http://www.londonmet.ac.uk/tltc/multimedia/multimedia_home.cfm.

The large file size of images, sound and video (in that order), discussed in 2.2, can be a greater problem when files are online. The time to download a file (from the server to a PC) can be long and irritating if students are working from home on a modem. You need to minimise file sizes by reducing the size, length and quality of the images and sound to that which is needed and no more.

There are broadly two ways to distribute audio or video resource files: downloading and streaming. Downloading is the norm. A file waits until you load them into the browser, whereupon they either appear within the browser or within reader software (e.g. Windows Media Player) that launches automatically to play it. Or you could download your own copy and play it later. A recent variation on downloading is podcasting (from *iPod*, the iconic Apple audio player, and *broadcasting*). It automates the downloading of files that are frequently changed or added, such as news items, typically as MP3 audio files. Podcasting is like asynchronous broadcasting; it is widely used for radio programmes (e.g. http://www.bbc.co.uk) but the technology can be used for educational content. You could manually download an audio file from a Web site (right-click on the file's web link) but podcasting allows you to subscribe to a *feed* Web site so that *aggregator* or *podcatcher* software on your PC (e.g. iTunes or Juice) can maintain a list of your subscriptions to such podcast feeds and then automatically download them for you as new items become available. That is, the podcast client software collects content to which you have subscribed. If you wish, it removes it from your computer once it has been played so it does not accumulate. The subscription system is known as Really Simple Syndication and is displayed as an orange RSS button on Web pages. RSS is not just for audio podcasts, it is used for subscriptions to news as text and images files.

Once the audio files are on your PC they can be copied to an iPod or other audio player and listened to anywhere, or played on a PC with Windows Media Player, for example. The technology is flexible. The audio could be educational content and your students could subscribe to a news feed on your course web site. Audio files and podcasting have a growing number of uses in education, such as course announcements, topic guides or even lectures, and will be especially useful for dyslexic students (Swain, 2006) or blind students.

The alternative distribution method is streaming, especially for audio and video files (ClickandGo, 2002, Shephard, 2003). Here, the local player software plays a file as it continuously arrives from the server. After a short delay to establish a few seconds of data in a buffer, a large file can be played without waiting for it to download. On the other hand, you do not have a local copy of it afterwards (unless you use 'ripper' software to capture it). This is essentially broadcasting over the internet, and the Web server needs to be capable of delivering the resource file in this way, so you must consult your technical support staff for advice. Internet 'radio stations' stream sound and may require a particular player (e.g. Winamp for streaming MP3 files).

Online presentations can take various forms. Software packages can create online presentations that include text, audio, video, and slides. They may add to existing

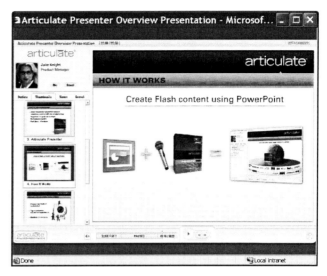

Figure 13 Online presentation in Flash created with Articulate using a PowerPoint presentation

presentations by dividing the screen into windows for a talking head, slides, outlines, text or quizzes (e.g. Boxmind, see Joiner *et al.*, 2003; sofTV.net, see Figure 13). Others (e.g. Impatica, Articulate) compress PowerPoint so that it can be easily distributed on the Internet and be played on Java- or Flash-enabled PCs or hand held devices, without needing the PowerPoint software. However, complete, if modest, online lectures can be created with PowerPoint alone. It is easy to include audio and video in PowerPoint slides, and to add an audio narration to each slide while sitting at your desk with a microphone. Therefore, think hard before investing training and money in additional software: if file size is not a problem, there is probably no need for anything other than making your PowerPoint files available, and directing students who do not own a copy to the free PowerPoint viewer (search http://www.microsoft.com for ppviewer.exe).

Some iPods and other mobile players can show still images and video, so in future we can expect to be able to create presentation podcasts and videos for mobile learners.

Such 'packaged lectures' are unlikely to be valuable in blended courses on campus but they may be of use in distance learning courses. They are more flexible to use than analogue videos of presentations and easier to distribute to students, although file size may be an issue depending on the bandwidth of the students' connections. If you simply add a narration to existing presentation slides, they may need little extra time to produce. However, on a blended course, live presentations can have the added value of student activity and interactivity (see 3.3), which cannot be packaged.

A further reason for using multimedia content is to increase the variety of media carrying the same message. Web sites, tutorials and other learning resources should be designed to accommodate learners with varying learning styles (Valley, 1997; Ford and Chen, 2001; Baldwin and Sabry, 2003). One dimension of difference is the preference for text or images. Some students (*visualisers* or *imagers*) think more visually and appreciate pictures, while others (*verbalisers*) prefer text (Riding, 1996; Riding and Raynor, 1998). This is a continuum rather than a dichotomy. Verbalisers appreciate verbal versions of pictorial material. So if you provide an image, sound or video file you should provide a text description or transcription linked nearby on the page. This is helpful to some students and essential to others with visual disabilities. (Within Web pages there is a specific mechanism – ALT text – to add a text label to every image, and all images should have one.) Conversely, visualisers need pictorial forms of verbal/textual information, and concrete analogies of abstract ideas (Riding, 1996 p. 22 ff). Video can provide both verbal and visual information simultaneously. Providing a variety of modes of presentation will help your students, with their variety of learning styles (e.g. Riding and Grimley, 1999).

Another dimension of differences in learning styles is the continuum between *wholists*, who prefer to organise information into wholes but have difficulty seeing the parts, and *serialists* (or *analytics*), who are good at seeing the parts but have difficulty integrating them (Riding, 1996). Wholists need *organisers*, such as telling them what you are going to tell them, or a pictorial map of a topic to indicate its parts and structure. Structural indicators such as a hierarchical content map and section numbers will help. Serialists tend to see one detail at a time and need an overview or summary to help them integrate the details into a whole. Mind maps are such a pictorial overview (section 2.3).

If a mind map can be used as a graphical menu – a clickable 'image map' – it can become part of your Web's navigation system as well as being content, part of the user interface. Other uses of images to help students navigate Webs include logos and icons. The two navigation problems for Web users can be summarised as, Where am I? and, Where is it? A logo for an institution or a course reminds students of the Web site they are using – where they are. An icon (a small, clickable image) can help them select the correct link to a document they want. The three important things about designing Web navigation are consistency, consistency, and consistency. Web sites should be easy to navigate if students are to find what they need easily. Part of 'usability' (or user-friendliness, if you like) is learnability. For example, students cannot learn what an icon means for navigation (where it will take them) unless it always has the same meaning. Choose your icons carefully: what information for navigation do they contain? Will

the students guess what the image signifies? In a virtual learning environment (VLE), icons are available for different types of links: to documents, Web sites, discussions, and so on. It may be possible for you to use alternative, or even custom-made, icons but stop! Are you just creating an additional learning task for no good reason? There is an advantage for learnability if the same icons are used consistently across all the courses an individual takes. Choose your navigation graphics for usability rather than aesthetic appeal (to you).

Another use of images with large student groups is the teacher's mug-shot! Especially where a large course has multiple teachers, believe it or not, some students do not know their teacher's name, nor would they recognise them in the corridor. Teaching should be a relationship, and an online mug-shot and biopic of each teacher helps to personalise it.

The number of technologies and file types that can be used for multimedia in Web pages continues to grow, for commercial reasons. Typically, we don't need them in education. Let's consider the types of files and technologies to use for course documents. You cannot assume your students' PCs have the software applications your PC has – because your pages 'work' on your PC does not mean they will do so on theirs. Simple Web pages (of HTML) should be readable in any browser on any PC, along with images in .gif or .jpg format. However, are you, in fact, writing technically simple pages? If you use an authoring tool (e.g. FrontPage, Dreamweaver) it may be using technologies in your pages that you are not aware of. You should control the Web technologies it is employing, using the minimum technologies required. Using more complex technologies will make pages slower to load and more prone to errors, especially with older browsers and equipment, and may make no significant improvement to the pages. I recommend disabling frames, ActiveX controls, Java, and CSS2 style sheets but retaining JavaScript and CSS1. (CSS – cascading style sheets – adds to the ability of HTML to format Web pages.)

Documents linked from Web pages do not have to be HTML documents. If you have existing documents, for example in MS Office formats (.doc, .ppt, .xls), you can put them directly on the Web (or VLE) but you should be sure that your students' PCs can display them. There is free reader software for these file types on the http://www.microsoft.com Web site and you should provide a link to them. An alternative for Word (.doc) documents is to save them in Rich Text Format (.rtf). This is readable in Word and other word processors, it retains the document formatting, and it has the added advantage that it cannot carry Word macro viruses. You could also save a Word document as a Web page. There are various options available: choose the ones compatible with the oldest browsers to maximise compatibility. (Some options produce not one file but a folder of many small files just to display one document.

This introduces an extra element of risk for student use. To avoid it, in later versions of MS Word, *Save As* the file type *Web Page Filtered* to minimise the size and complexity of the file.) You can also convert one Word document into a Web site of linked pages with, for example, CourseGenie.

Do you need to learn to use a Web authoring tool? Probably not. Once you experience the benefits of technology, it is all too easy to waste time mastering software to produce online resources. Just because, for example, Dreamweaver is the most popular Web editor for commercial environments does not mean that you need it, or can justify the time needed to learn it. Using a VLE will be easier, if one is available. Then, ask what can be done with the tools with which you are already familiar, such as your word processor? If you need it, can you get more complex work done by a media support unit? Can you get advice from your information services or staff development unit on the tools with the maximum payoff and the minimum effort? For example, CourseGenie will generate Web sites or VLE sites from structured Word documents and the concept mapping software MindSmart will generate Web sites with an image of the concept map as a graphical menu. Your institution may have site licenses for software that local experts think suitable; consider them carefully before using alternatives.

Electronic resources such as images, Web pages or streamed video can be converted into 'learning objects' that can be shared and reused in new contexts if they are labelled in standard ways to enable searching. Two such standards are IMS Learning Design and SCORM. VLEs should support such standards so that you can import content from elsewhere, generated in other systems.

4.3 Individual use of online tools and resources

The good news is that everything is available online. The bad news is that everything is available online.

It is hard to imagine now, but not so long ago the usual problem was that little useful information was available electronically, online. Now we have the opposite problem of online information overload: most simple searches of the Web generate thousands of 'hits' and more documents of potential relevance than a student could find in most libraries.

Some academic journals are freely available on the Web and your institution probably subscribes to others. It may also subscribe to electronic books such as the netlibrary service. This allows you embed Web addresses in online reading lists or task descriptions, to give easy access to the books and articles you recommend. Nonetheless, students will use Web search engines. Currently most students (and staff!) start their online searching with Google (http://www.google.co.uk)

(Griffiths and Brophy, 2002). Good advice for students about searching the Web would include:

1   Learn how to use the advanced searching features of any search engine, to focus the search and get more relevant results

2   Use specialist search engines; for example, Google Scholar (http://scholar.google.com) only searches academic materials

3   Use academic portals such as Intute (http://www.intute.ac.uk – (previously the Resource Discovery Network) to access quality-assured resources.

With a little practice, finding more relevant Web pages is not difficult, but then students need the 'information literacy' skills to evaluate the academic value of what they find (Bostock, 2001; Murray *et al.*, 2005). A generic tutorial about the Internet, including this evaluation, is TONIC (http://www.netskills.ac.uk/TONIC) and another (my favourite) is Internet Detective (http://www.vts.intute.ac.uk/detective). The Virtual Training Suite is a collection of over 60 subject-specific tutorials (at http://www.intute.ac.uk) – all free.

Computer-based tutorials, in general, are a type of specialist, structured resource for learning, an interactive alternative to reading a document. They are arguably a surrogate teacher, which places them in cell B5 in the organiser, but they are mentioned here for convenience. In a tutorial, content is divided into small chunks and progressing through the pages typically depends on answering objective tests correctly. It makes little difference if a tutorial is on a CD-ROM, or other local disk, or online on a Web site. Creating such a tutorial is not trivial and should not be undertaken lightly. Like computer-based testing (which they often include), tutorials are likely to be worthwhile developing only if there are large numbers of students using them to learn simple, stable content. Although a tutorial could be created in a generic authoring tool such as MS FrontPage, it is easier with specialist software tools such as Calnet (http://www.webecon.bris.ac.uk/calnet/) or Macromedia's Authorware. On the other hand, if you can give your students access to professionally developed tutorials they can be a valuable resource. For example, Winecon is a tutorial for first year undergraduate economics (Soper and MacDonald, 1994; Brooksbank *et al.*, 1998, http://www.winecon.com/). Computer-based tutorials can certainly be as effective as traditional face-to-face teaching (e.g. Johnson *et al.*, 1997).

A second type of structured resource is a simulation. Simulations are representations by software of important aspects of the real world phenomenon being studied; they are usefully simplified models of the world, often representing their results graphically. Like tutorials, they take much time and expertise to create; don't even consider it. However, if you are able to use an existing one that fits your course, they can be most valuable to student learning. One exception to the general warning of not attempting to create simulations is using spreadsheets to model cases or concepts in some numerical subjects. If you can provide your students with spreadsheet models which they can use, by varying inputs to observe outputs and by examining the formulae constituting the model, it will certainly support their learning. Large tutorials such as Winecon include simulations as part of their instruction.

A Web client (browser) is an essential tool for most online resources. Students need to be able to set up their browser properly (for example, in Internet Explorer 6.0), including:

1   Being able to adjust the text size (View, Text size)

2   Switching on some of the Accessibility options such as 'ignore font sizes' (Tools, Internet options, General, Accessibility)

3   Saving valuable Web addresses – Uniform Resource Locators (URLs) – in the browser's Favourites or Bookmarks, and organising them into topic folders

4   Exporting your Favourites occasionally to a file in My Documents (with File, Export), where it will be backed up (section 1.5)

5   Learning how to give a Web site as a reference (e.g. Walker and Taylor, 1998).

Amongst the Web resources that need cautious evaluation as academic resources are public blogs (4.4) and wikis (6.1), but both can be valuable as tools for individual or group writing, respectively.

4.4   Student self assessment

Higher Education aspires to developing students into independent lifelong learners. As feedback on performance is necessary for learning, independent learners must be able to assess themselves to give themselves feedback. Alongside this aspiration is the growing dissatisfaction with the degree classification system and the drive for providing students with a richer record of their achievements to take to prospective employers. All UK Universities are required to support students' personal development planning (PDP). This typically uses a portfolio or 'progress file' to collect evidence of abilities, plans, and personal reflections.

'the Progress File will … provide each student with a transcript – a record of their learning and achievement and a means by which the student can monitor, build and reflect upon their personal development. [PDP is] a structured and supported process undertaken by an individual to reflect upon their own learning, performance and / or achievement and to plan for their personal, educational and career development.' (Guide to Curriculum Design: Personal Development Planning (2002) on the Higher Education Academy Web)

Figure 14 A simple blog

Such PDP portfolios can be paper-based but there are advantages in Web-based e-portfolios, for example, PebblePad or Turnitin's Digital Portfolio. Accessible from any networked PC, they allow students to add their own documents and allow the institution to add student grades and policy documents, for example concerning the generic skills in its courses. The portfolio contents can be downloaded in a portable format at will. Online portfolios can encourage students in the processes of PDP: planning; learning through experience; recording; reviewing, reflecting; and evaluating one's performance to start a new planning cycle. As a teacher or personal tutor you will need to be familiar with the PDP support framework within your institution, and with any software it uses.

While PDP portfolios are owned by the student, not assessed, and are based on a whole programme, smaller portfolios including electronic ones can also be used within courses as part of student-assessed work. An e-portfolio could be a collection of documents and reflective statements, or it could use a discussion board topic or a personal folder in a VLE. A blog could also be used as a small portfolio or journal for reflective writing and self assessment. Blogs (Web logs) are online diaries or journals, and writing one can be a learning activity. Blogs are a simple way of creating and adding to a Web page without having to use a Web authoring software tool. The blog Web site provides all the facilities for creating new text and maintaining the blog, for example MSN Spaces, Blogspot (see Figure 14), or in some VLEs. Blogs on the commercial Web sites can be public, or be private to the author or to a group. Within a course, a teacher could also use a blog as a way maintaining course information on the Web, as an alternative to maintaining a Web site with a Web authoring tool or a VLE. Students can write their own blogs as reflective diaries, and being online allows them to be shared at will with a teacher or their peers, who could be allowed to add their own comments to it. This is perhaps a simpler technology for the purpose than alternatives like using a Web discussion board. A blog can be used as an e-portfolio (4.4) or collection of documents. For example, a 'patchwork text' (Winter, 2003) is a type of written assignment consisting of a series of small pieces, later stitched together with some reflective writing. These pieces could be messages on a blog, with a final reflective message.

4.5 Further reading

Accessibility issues
For accessibility issues for VLEs, see http://www.durham.ac.uk/alert

TechDis is a support service for technology and disability. They recently published a Staff Pack for developers and teachers, see http://www.techdis.ac.uk

The DEMOS project *'developed an online learning package aimed specifically at academic staff and examined the issues faced by disabled students in higher education'* it says on: http://jarmin.com/demos/

The Lexia font is available free from K-TYPE, http://www.k-type.com/index.html

Bostock, S. J. (2002) 'Designing Web sites that are accessible to all', *Educational Developments* 3.3, 18-19, also at http://www.keele.ac.uk/depts/aa/landt /lt/docs/review_web_accessibility.htm

Further links on Web accessibility are at http://www.keele.ac.uk/depts/aa/landt

The Acrobat Reader for .pdf files is at http://www.adobe.co.uk/products/acrobat/readermain.html

Learning resources, learning objects and repositories
A recent thoughtful review: Allison Littlejohn and Lou McGill (2004) 'Effective resources for e-learning', report for the JISC e-learning and pedagogy research study, http://www.jisc.ac.uk/uploaded_documents/detailed%20 report%20-resources-first%20draft_lou_mcgill.doc

Lukasiak, J., Agostinho, S., Bennet, S., Harper, B., Lockyer, L. and Powley, B. (2005) 'Learning objects and learning designs: an integrated system for reusable, adaptive and shareable learning content', ALT-J, 13 (2): 151-169.

Malcolm, M. (2005) 'The exercise of objects: issues in resource reusability and reuse', *British Journal of Technology*, 36 (1): 33-41.

'Jorum is a free online repository service for teaching and support staff in UK Further and Higher Education Institutions'. If your institution is registered with Jorum you can use your Athens login to browse the repository, download materials and re-purpose them for your

teaching. If you wish to contribute materials, contact your institutional Jorum representative, http://www.jorum.ac.uk/

The Moving Image Gateway (MIG) is a good place to look for video clips. It *'collects together websites that relate to moving images and sound and their use in higher and further education'*, http://www.bufvc.ac.uk/gateway/

'The HERMES database provides details of over 25,000 audio-visual programmes in distribution throughout the UK', http://www.bufvc.ac.uk/databases/index.html

'The Resource Discovery Network is the UK's free national gateway to Internet resources for the learning, teaching and research community', http://www.rdn.ac.uk/

The Technical Advisory Service for Images *'have collected details of a wide range of digital image collections and projects and compiled an Image Sites collection'*, it says on their Web site; they have advice documents and you can search their databases at http://www.tasi.ac.uk/

Patchwork text
Innovations in Education and Teaching International (May 2003) Issue 2, volume 40, is a special issue on the subject.

Learning styles and using technology
British Journal of Technology (2003), Special issue 32 (4), on Individual differences in Web-based instruction.

Sadler-Smith, E. and Smith, P. J. (2004) 'Strategies for accommodating individuals' styles and preferences in flexible learning programmes', British Journal of Technology, 35 (4): 395-412.

(All Web sites accessed on 23 December 2005)

5 Online teacher-student interactivity

Computer networks can provide a communication channel for interactivity between students or with a teacher, in groups or one-to-one. This type of computer application has been called Computer Media Communication (CMC). The multimedia and storage capabilities of computers allow a number of possibilities:

1   The communication mode can be as text, pictures, audio or video

2   The timing can be synchronous (in real time) or asynchronous (stored and collected)

3   Communication can be one-to-one (private), one-to-many (e.g. announcement), many-to-many (e.g. discussion), or many-to-one (e.g. assignment submission)

4   Communication can be read-only (e.g. an online notice-board, or 'lurkers' who read but do not contribute to discussion), write-only (e.g. assignment submission), or read-and-write (e.g. a structured discussion or e-mail).

Not all the possible combinations of these modes are used in education but a few are well established and others are novel experiments. Most services useful for teacher-student communication are also useful for student-student communication but they are split, for convenience, across this chapter and the next. This chapter therefore discusses online communication by e-mail and also computer assisted assessment, which is essentially feedback by proxy from a teacher to students, even though it is often experienced as an individual activity (Organiser cell C5).

5.1 E-mail

Most of us make regular use of e-mail and some of us suffer from e-mail overload. E-mail is a good way of sending information to one or many students, to have one-to-one student interactions, such as dealing with problems, or answering questions, and to have planned interactions like project supervision or mentoring (Paulsen, 1995). E-mail is less good for many-to-many discussions because the number of messages can grow dramatically, they are mixed with other e-mail, messages can lack context unless the writers are disciplined in making clear the links between messages, and everyone must store their own copies systematically. So, for many-to-many discussions, 'computer conferencing' is a better environment (see 6.1).

E-mail addresses can be problematical. You could receive an e-mail from an address you do not know (e.g. hotbabe@yahoo.com) asking for a meeting. Is this your student? Your institution may already have a policy of using only institutional addresses. If not, you should ask your students to give you their e-mail addresses in advance so you can check incoming e-mail against the list. Your institution may provide you with a group

address (or alias) for all the students on a course, generated from central student records. If not, you will need your own list to be able to send them e-mail. You could type all the addresses into the To: line on your e-mail software but with many addresses this is error-prone. It would be better to make a text file of the addresses (with e.g. Windows Notepad), with one address per line. You can then paste the list into your software when sending an e-mail. Your e-mail client on your PC (e.g. Outlook, Eudora) may allow you to create a single name as a course alias. Another possibility is using a bulk mailer (e.g. Worldcast), which will pick up the list of addresses from your text file and send the same message to all of them.

To make it easier for you to manage course e-mails, tell students to put their course title or code in the message Subject. Save all messages in one folder per course. If you send important course messages by e-mail, place a copy of the message on the course Web site as a fall-back for students who do not read, or who lose, their e-mail. Your institution may have a policy on how long you should keep correspondence with students.

One classic e-mail trap is to reply to all recipients rather than just replying to the sender of a message. At worst, this might mean you sending a droll message concerning the Vice-Chancellor's dress sense to an old mate but mistakenly copying it to the whole institution. As embarrassing for a student may be your copying a personal reply to the whole class. *Always* check the recipients list before pressing the Send button! Also, if there is any chance a message may cause offence, sleep on it before sending.

It is important for students to know how often they should check their e-mail box and how often you will check yours. I commonly ask students to check at least once a week and promise to reply to messages within three days. Otherwise, you may get phone calls asking why you didn't already reply!

An insidious problem with asynchronous communications like e-mail is that, although the timing of reading and writing messages is flexible, it can be difficult to control the total time it consumes. Every individual message may be worthwhile and contribute to a student's learning experience, but at the expense of longer working hours for teachers. With a large course, how can you control the time you spend answering e-mails? Managing your time can help: reading e-mail only at certain times of the day and ruthlessly deleting without opening messages that are unlikely to be important (Figure 15). You must read all messages from students, obviously, but you can discourage unnecessary e-mails. An online question-and-answer discussion board (see 6.1) will allow other students to answer some questions before you need to. For questions you do answer by e-mail, add them to an anonymous frequently asked questions (FAQ) Web page and then you need not answer it again: tell students to check the discussion

Approaches that might aid the management of e-mail messages are:

1   Allocating sufficient time each day or week to read through and action e-mail messages

2   Prioritising which e-mail messages need to be dealt with first

3   Looking at the sender and the title to gauge the importance of the message

4   Flagging where you have been copied into e-mail messages.
    These messages are often only for informational purposes and do not require immediate/any action

5   Setting rules for incoming messages so they can automatically be put into folders

6   Using folders to group e-mail messages of a similar nature or subject together so they can be dealt with consecutively

7   Identifying e-mail messages that are records or need to be brought to other people's attention

8   Keeping e-mail messages in personal folders only for short-term personal information.
    E-mails that are required for longer purpose should be managed as records

9   Deleting e-mail messages that are kept elsewhere as records

10 Deleting e-mail messages that are no longer required for reference purposes from the in and out box.

Figure 15 Advice on managing e-mails from Russell (2004, p.20)

board or FAQ page before e-mailing you. It is easy to lose track of the staff time spent in online activity (although within a VLE this can be monitored). The purpose of technology is not to enable you to work longer! Try to be credited with working hours related to the number of students you teach rather than your scheduled face-to-face contact hours that omit online work.

You must manage your e-mail like any other data, keeping copies of all significant e-mail messages with students, incoming and outgoing. Configure your e-mail software to keep copies of outgoing e-mail. E-mails are disclosable under the UK Freedom of Information Act and are 'business records'. You will need e-mail folders (boxes) for different purposes, just as you have folders for files on your PC. If you collect your e-mail on a Windows PC, place your e-mail folders within My Documents so they are regularly backed-up with your other data. If you keep your incoming e-mail on a mail server, you can still organise it into folders but it should be backed-up for you.

Two reasons for e-mail overload are spam and lists. Spam e-mail is unsolicited commercial e-mail, most of it concerning pornography, financial scams or dubious products (Schott, 2006). Those sending it use software to harvest e-mail addresses from Web pages and e-mail lists, so be careful where you leave your e-mail address. Some commercial and institutional e-mail services scan incoming e-mail for spam and remove it, or flag it as likely spam to help you quickly delete it. Spam can be worse than a waste of time; it can contain links or attached files that might introduce viruses or other malicious software. Never click a link in a spam message even if it promises to unsubscribe you from a list (they lie!), and never open an attached file unless you know the sender.

E-mail lists are useful and seductively easy to join. Listservers are services that copy an e-mail from one person on the list to all the others on a list. Your e-mail may be placed on some lists in your institution. Other lists you can join, either at your institution or nationally or internationally. For example, JISCmail is a UK national service that maintains thousands of e-mail lists for UK academics, on a vast range of subjects. Joining and leaving lists can be done by e-mail, of course, but also by a Web interface, which is more convenient. The problem with lists is that they can generate a lot of e-mail unexpectedly, and it may no longer be of interest. Keep all messages from list managers carefully (in one folder) so that you can find the information on how to leave a list when its messages are no longer of interest. In addition to normal good practice in sending e-mail (netiquette), there are additional issues for lists. For example, conducting a private e-mail conversation on a list, especially a bad-tempered one, wastes the time of everyone else on the list. Messages that should be sent to the list manager are often wrongly sent to the whole list. Be careful when you post a message to a list if you don't want to irritate your network of peers.

Another issue for e-mail is multiple addresses and redirection. E-mail is only useful for communication if the recipient checks their mail. Redirection sends e-mail arriving at the inbox of one address to that of a different e-mail address. Students may need to use redirection if they don't want to read their institutional mailbox: they can redirect e-mails from it to their personal mailbox on a different mail server like Hotmail. If you have multiple e-mail addresses I recommend redirecting them all to one mailbox.

If your e-mail is downloaded onto your office desktop PC, and removed from the mail server, you have to be in the office to access it. If it is left on the server you may be able to access it through a Web interface (e.g. Webmail) from anywhere. The disadvantage is that for large amounts of e-mail a Web interface can be slower and less capable than e-mail software on a PC. Another possibility (that I use) is to download e-mail into an e-mail client on my laptop. E-mail can then be read and written anywhere, and e-mails can be received and sent whenever the laptop is connected to the Internet, in the office, through a modem or through public wireless connections (wifi). But take a break from it sometime! The beauty of e-mail is that it will wait for you.

Virtual learning environments (see chapter 7) may have their own e-mail system. That makes it easy for you to e-mail student individuals and groups, but this e-mail system may or may not be connected to the students' normal Internet or institutional e-mail. Make sure students understand the extent to which the two systems are separate, and how they might reply to you.

5.2 Computer Assisted Assessment

It may seem odd to include online assessment under teacher-student interactivity. However, giving formative assessment is teaching and, for students, summative assessment underpins much else in a course. So assessment is a major type of student-teacher interaction.

When computer assisted assessment (CAA) is discussed it is usually in the form of objective tests such as multiple choice questions (MCQs). Objective tests are those that can be marked automatically by a computer with simple matching rules – the correct box is ticked; the correct word is typed, and so on. Human judgment is not needed. Figure 16 lists some common forms.

Why would you use such objective tests? Two common reasons are: summative, to reduce the marking and grading load in large student cohorts; and formative, to provide more formative feedback more quickly than a teacher can do manually.

Formative assessment

Students often get less feedback on their performance than they need; more formative assessment would help learning (e.g. Peat and Franklin, 2002). Objective tests can provide feedback in addition to the correctness of an answer: they can provide specific feedback on each answer given, and a source of further reading that would address particular mistakes. Formative tests can be re-used repeatedly by students until they gain high marks. Indeed, a problem with a small minority of students is that they can become obsessive users until they achieve full marks (Bostock, 2004). For most students, formative tests provide evidence of their progress on a course – which is motivating – and feedback on their weaknesses. This is no extra work for the teacher, once the test is in place.

Note that for formative purposes it is not necessary for the CAA software to validate users, store answers, or create reports and grades for teachers. Users can be anonymous and software can be simpler (e.g. Hot Potatoes): individual Web pages where the marking and feedback is generated in the page by JavaScript.

Summative assessment

Summative objective tests can be delivered by a computer network but they can also be completed on paper and then marked by hand (perhaps by someone else – it requires no subject expertise) or by a machine. Optical mark recognition (OMR) can detect a mark in a

---

1   True/false

2   Multiple choice: 4-6 answers from which one must be chosen

3   Multiple responses: 4-6 answers from which one or more can be selected; the correct answer is a particular pattern of selection. E.g. 'Which one or more of the following statements is true?'

4   Fill in the blank: some text is presented with words or phrases missing, which must be typed. E.g. 'Mary had a little lamb, its _____ was white as snow.' The typed answer is matched with *fleece*

5   Jumbled sentence: text is presented with words or phrases missing, and for each gap there is a drop-down list of options. E.g. 'In a right-angle triangle, the <option list> on the <option list> is equal to the sum of the <option list> on the other two sides.'

6   Matching lists: there are two lists and each item in one list must be matched to one in the other list. E.g. lists of countries and capital cities

7   Numerical: typed answers are evaluated as number values, not as text. The questions might be generated from expressions so that the question (and correct answer) is different every time

8   Image hotspots: a click on an area of an image identifies an answer

9   Drag-and-drop: graphical objects are dragged across the screen and dropped on other objects.

Figure 16 Common Types of Objective Questions

box. Either the answers are completed on special sheets with a matrix of boxes in standard positions or the OMR machine may have software that can be trained to use an individual question paper with boxes in unique positions. The latter is easier for students but more work for the teacher or technician.

More usually, CAA involves delivering the tests to the screen, where students complete them. There are obvious advantages: questions can be stored in question banks and re-used, selected in random order or according to criteria such as difficulty. The software can produce standard reports of student grades and of the characteristics of the questions that will help improve them. The disadvantages include having to learn how to use particular software, such as QuestionMark or the assessment features of a VLE, and having to enter the question and answer data into the software. This last chore need not be done online; a package like Respondus allows you to create questions onsite suitable for different delivery systems.

If you have not used CAA before, it might be worth a trial run of objective testing on paper with manual marking before committing additional time to creating the tests in software.

Following a review of the literature on innovative assessment (much of it computer-assisted) and student motivation (Bostock, 2004), my conclusions included:

1   Innovative assessment can provide timely feedback to support learning

2   Students will be unfamiliar with it and so need guidelines, clarification, instruction and practice

3   Clarity of assessed outcomes and criteria are always desirable but are essential for innovative assessment

4   Diversity of assessment will be fair to the widening diversity of students

5   If novelty is introduced in small amounts it will reduce student anxiety and the risks to success

The amount and mix of summative assessments in any one course must not be too complex.

Validity

Assessments need to be valid, reliable, and cost-effective. Validity means they actually test what they are supposed to. It is a common problem in many types of assessment (computerised or not) that they actually test a 'shadow' version of the learning outcomes. For example, while the learning outcomes refer to skills such as analysis and design, assessments may actually test the ability to remember a description of analysis and design.

What types of learning outcomes can be tested objectively? One problem is that the right answers must be known in advance, so creative solutions cannot be tested. Only correct answers, rather than good methods, can be assessed. To use the six categories of Bloom

(1956), it is easier to test recall and comprehension and harder to test more complex learning such as application, analysis, synthesis and evaluation by any means, and particularly so by objective tests (Peat, 2000, p.54). Some argue that it is possible (e.g. Bull and McKenna, 2003), but it will certainly take more effort to design valid tests of these 'higher order' skills. This cost must be weighed in the decision to use objective tests.

Valid multiple choice tests are difficult to write. It is difficult to think of plausible but wrong answers ('distracters'), perhaps because they should be common student misconceptions and we don't share them. Poorly written MCQs allow student tactics to improve guessing. Biggs (2003, p.180) lists some of them: never choose facetious or jargon-ridden options; eliminate all the options you can, then guess; and if one option elicits a faint glow of recognition, choose it. If MCQs allow such tactics to be rewarded, they have failed as valid assessments.

One response to guessing is negative marking. With MCQs and some other question types, random answers would, on average, give a positive total score, thus giving weak students free marks. Therefore, wrong answers should be given a negative score to counterbalance the positive scores from chance correct answers. The principle is that, if all answers were chosen (i.e. any one at random, with equal chance), the mark would be zero. For example, if one answer from five is correct in an MCQ, this could score +4 and each wrong answer would score -1 (+4-1-1-1-1=0). Unanswered questions score zero. The mechanics of arranging for the positive and negative marks for each option will vary in software packages. That will require training or reading the manual. Negative marking may mean that weak students do badly in MCQs, even scoring below zero. A negative overall test score should be adjusted to zero before it is used for wider purposes. More sophisticated systems allow students to indicate their confidence in their answer, higher positive marks for confident right answers but higher negative marks for confident but wrong answers. Students do not generally like negative marking (for obvious reasons, they lose free marks) so you must explain the reasons for it.

Although the marking is automatic, the pass mark is an educational decision. While grading an essay provides a qualitative judgment against a set of criteria (even if the criteria are left implicit), objective tests tell us how *many* things were remembered or understood. Should 100% be required? Or some other figure? There is no particular reason to use the usual threshold of 40% or 50%. It is an educational decision, related to the aims of the course. Similarly, we should not combine arithmetically the results of objective assessments with those of other assessments by averaging their percentages, unless their pass marks happen to be the same. The algorithm for combining the scores of objective tests with other, qualitative judgments is an educational decision based on the importance of various learning outcomes and the purposes of the course. For example, achieving 80% on an MCQ test might be a threshold requirement before the grade on an essay was used as the overall course grade.

Apart from reporting on the grades of students, software like QuestionMark and VLEs like WebCT will generate reports for teachers about the questions themselves. The following statistics for *each question* are useful:

1 Average score for each question, indicating its difficulty

2 Facility: the proportion of students giving the correct answer as a proportion of all students; again, indicating question difficulty

3 Discrimination: how many of the best third of the students got a question right, minus how many of the worst third of the students got a question right, divided by the number of students in a third. (Best and worst are defined as the students with the highest and lowest marks in this test.) This value has a scale from -1 through zero to +1 (although it might be presented differently in some software). The higher the number, the more discriminating is a question. A low number means that the question was answered equally well by students who did well overall and by those who did badly overall; unlikely for a valid question, so the question should be checked in case it is ambiguous or misleading

4 Frequency of each answer to a question: if a question has suspect validity, the frequency of specific wrong answers may indicate why. For example, one distracter may be ambiguous.

Such statistics may help detect and confirm questions with poor validity that should be dropped or improved. On the other hand, validity is ultimately about the fitness for assessing the intended learning outcomes, so the statistics can only be a guide. Although, as part of test development, you should get a colleague to take the test, it is not until students take it that their mistakes can indicate any problems with validity.

Reliability

The marking of objective tests is completely reliable, barring equipment failures, but what about the reliability of the answering process? Computer-delivered tests can be made quite robust against cheating. The software for summative testing must run on a server, probably a Web server, which delivers questions to the screens of students logged in as identifiable individuals and stores their answers securely. Questions can be presented in random order and with randomly ordered options. Summative tests can use booked PC laboratories and the software can reject attempts to login from other rooms. It can require a special password only announced at the start of the test by an invigilator.

The software needed for summative testing is more complex and robust than that needed for formative testing. Multiple simultaneous users will put a high load on the server. You will have to arrange the use of PC rooms and discuss with the system's administrator the load your test will put on the server. You need to be confident it will cope with the number of simultaneous users, and have a paper backup in case it doesn't.

Cost-effectiveness

Objective tests shift the teaching workload from the marking of individual students' work to the initial design of tests that can later be marked automatically. Staff time is more costly than software and equipment, but you obviously need access to these. Under what circumstances is using CAA likely to be cost-effective, in terms of getting a return on the up-front investment in time and equipment? A net saving in time is likely after two or more years if: the student cohort is large (100+); the questions test low-level learning outcomes and are therefore easy to write and likely to be valid; the content is stable, to minimise the need for maintenance of the question bank; and you have the support of colleagues and management so that the results will be acceptable and your workload will benefit once the investment has been made. A good candidate would be factual knowledge in a large, introductory course.

You may be able to use or adapt a question bank from the support Web site of a textbook you adopt, or from a subject-based consortium such as those organised by some Subject Centres of the HE Academy (http://www.heacademy.ac.uk).

One final issue about objective tests, especially summative ones, is perhaps esoteric but nonetheless serious: objective tests indicate an impoverished theory of knowledge. Degree level learning outcomes should include an appreciation of the uncertainty, ambiguity and limits of knowledge (QAA, 2000). However, *'when used exclusively, MCQs send all the wrong messages to students'* (Biggs, 2003, p.181): that knowledge is just a set of facts; that some answers are right, some are wrong, and that what matters is knowing which are correct. For this reason amongst others, summative objective tests should only be a part of the assessment mix.

Surveys

Forms on a Web page can collect typed answers to open questions. These Web forms can be delivered from an ordinary Web server or from a VLE or from CAA software. The answers are stored, or sent by e-mail, for human inspection.

Web forms are very useful for student evaluations of courses (e.g. Moss and Hendry, 2002). Finding the contact time to have students complete paper evaluation forms is difficult, and asking students to complete them 'later' usually gives a poor response rate. The data must then be transcribed for analysis. A Web form can be presented whenever you wish, or be accessible throughout the course. It will capture the data electronically so that you can load it into a spreadsheet for analysis. If the form is a survey within a VLE, the VLE will tabulate it for you. On a Web server, anonymous submission of a form means the users are not tracked, making it difficult to require submission, but a survey form in a VLE will report which students have completed it without identifying them as the authors of particular forms, retaining their essential anonymity.

Administrative support for assessment

Online support for teacher assessment adds some advantages over stand-alone software (section 3.4). A Web-based VLE or assessment service like Turnitin can:

1 Accept electronic student submissions within specified dates

2 Support mark-up, grading and commenting on the assignment

3 Integrate with online detection of plagiarism or collusion (see next section)

4 Record the grades in an online grade book

5 Release the comments and marks to the student when appropriate.

Assessment of the student contributions to online discussions can be assisted in a VLE by its presenting on the screen a summary and a transcript of the contributions of each individual, alongside a form for the assessor that sends grades to the grade book.

5.3 Plagiarism detection

First, a warning: the use of plagiarism detection software must not be allowed to degrade the assessment process into a cynical game of students trying to cheat by re-using text without acknowledgement and teachers trying to catch them. The main emphases should be on valuing and supporting scholarship in writing and other work. Nonetheless, students new to university work in the UK may not understand what is expected in terms of writing in 'their own words', or the importance of accuracy in quotation and citation. Also, an occasional cynical or desperate student may decide to cheat. Plagiarism and collusion must not succeed if we are to protect the value of our degrees for other students; a culture of tolerating plagiarism will undermine the motivation of honest students. The knowledge that student assignments can be scanned for plagiarism (more accurately, for text matches) will be an additional deterrent. Such software can be a useful aid in clarifying whether an academic offence has been committed.

The general level of plagiarism may have increased; it is difficult to know. At least one form of plagiarism *has* increased in recent years: copying and pasting from Web documents. However, the availability to students of many electronic sources is now balanced by the ability of search engines to help teachers to find documents with matching sections of text. For detecting collusion, software can check for matching text within a cohort of assignments far more effectively than could a teacher. There is no technology that literally detects plagiarism or collusion; matching text could, after all, be properly

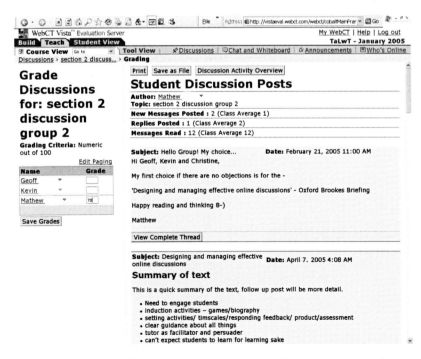

Figure 17 Grading a WebCT online discussion (with surnames erased)

quoted and cited. Furthermore, the plagiarism of images or of ideas cannot be detected. Nonetheless, software can scan student assignments for the presence of text that should be cited, which can then easily be checked manually. Let's consider the two most useful software tools.

In the past, a marker might become suspicious of a text passage in student work for reasons such as unusual vocabulary, changing format, or questionable relevance. If a suspicious phrase is chosen, of up to ten words, and placed in the Google search engine within quotes, there is a good chance that any Web documents containing the phrase will be found. This is quick and effective as a reactive check for a possible Web source after a suspicion is aroused, although several phrases may need to be tried.

Other plagiarism detection software can be used to scan the whole text of an individual assignment or proactively screen the whole text of a cohort of assignments. Turnitin is the chosen software of the UK Plagiarism Detection Service (http://www.submit.ac.uk). Your institution may subscribe to it. It matches student assignments against (i) the public Web, (ii) its own cache copies of pages that have since been removed from the Web, (iii) against other student work in the cohort submitted with it – collusion, (iv) all other student work submitted by other UK institutions, and (v) the electronic sources of some textbooks. After each assignment is submitted, a report is generated identifying the total percentage of text shared with other sources, what those sources are, and the text that matches each. There is a demonstration of such a report on the Web site, and a link to the Plagiarism Advisory Service which has many useful resources.

For any software plagiarism detection, an electronic copy of the work is needed. Online submission is easier than having students submitting discs. Students can submit assignments directly to the PDS (but not necessarily see their own plagiarism report), from where teachers can download them. Alternatively, VLEs have facilities for electronic submission, and are be able to link to the PDS so that plagiarism reports can be generated without a separate submission.

5.4 Further reading

Plagiarism
Carroll, J. and Appleton, J. (2001) *Plagiarism: A Good Practice Guide*, JISC/Oxford Brookes University, http://www.jisc.ac.uk/uploaded_documents/brookes.pdf

Carroll, J. (2002) *A Handbook for Deterring Plagiarism in Higher Education*, Oxford: Oxford Centre for Staff and Learning Development

The JISC Plagiarism Advisory Service has many useful resources and links: http://www.jiscpas.ac.uk/

Further links on plagiarism prevention and detection are at http://www.keele.ac.uk/depts/aa/landt/links/plagiarism.htm

Computer Assisted Assessment:
The Computer Assisted Assessment Centre Web is archived at http://caacentre.lboro.ac.uk/

Bull, J. and McKenna, C. (2003) *A Blueprint for Computer-assisted Assessment*, London: RoutledgeFalmer (the best introduction).

Conole, G. and Warburton, B. (2005) 'A review of computer-assisted assessment', *ALT-J*, 13 (1): 17-31.

ALT-J, 12 (3) is a special issue on CAA.

The Hot Potatoes homepage is http://www.halfbakedsoftware.com

Cost-effectiveness is discussed in: Loewenberger, P. and Bull, J. (2003) 'Cost effectiveness analysis of computer-based assessment', *ALT-J*, 11 (2): 23-45.

Further links on CAA are at: http://www.keele.ac.uk/depts/aa/landt/links/assessment.htm

6   Online student interactivity

This chapter discusses online student interactivity (Organiser cell C4).

6.1   Discussion and collaboration

While online resources are the most obvious way of supporting the 'delivery' aspects of teaching (4.1, 4.2), shared asynchronous text and online collaboration often support the 'discussion' aspects of learning. Text discussion boards have been termed 'bulletin boards' or 'computer conferencing' but neither is an accurate metaphor. The experience of discussion boards is not like a face-to-face conference or like reading a notice-board of announcements. They are like a structured, group, e-mail box. Only a single copy of every message exists, in one, shared space where everyone in a group can see them whenever they wish. The software keeps track of which messages have been read and written by every member of the group, and when. Messages that are unread by each individual are highlighted (as 'new') for them to catch attention, but all messages are still available.

Messages are typically organised into virtual spaces usually called topics. Within a topic, each initial message, plus all the replies to it, forms a 'thread' (Figure 18). Threads typically share the same Subject header. This structuring is useful to provide a context for each new message: the development of discussion can be revisited at will. It does, however, require some self-discipline from every participant to place messages and replies in appropriate positions, and (as always) choose a helpful, descriptive message Subject. If your institution has a VLE, it undoubtedly includes a discussion board. If you have no local service, try the free service Basic Support for Cooperative Work (http://bscw.fit.fraunhofer.de/).

Some example teaching-learning activities that have been used in discussion boards are discussion groups, structured debates, role plays, brainstorming, team projects, visiting experts and snowballing - starting with small groups given a task, merging these into larger ones to compare results, and then ending with a plenary. Some of these activities are supported by the ability of members to upload files of documents and images, for others to see and comment on.

Teaching-learning activities using discussion boards need to be designed in advance. Here are some issues to consider (CSALT, 2001):

1   Group size: large groups can easily be divided into small ones in an online environment. What is the optimum group size? It will depend on such things as what tasks the groups are performing, the period available and the frequency of students connecting, how verbose the students are, and the usability of the software. Try to envisage how many messages will be written per week in each group and how long that will take each student to read them all. If you are guessing, try groups of ten or twenty

2   Construction of the online space. Floor space in virtual rooms (topics) is free but how many rooms do you need? Apart from spaces for particular tasks or groups, there should generally be a space for socialising (the *Café*) so that it does not intrude inappropriately in working areas, and an area for practicing with the technology (the *Playpen* or *Sandpit*) where content is irrelevant. The number of discussion spaces needed will depend on how many tasks are set, how heterogeneous the contents are, and how disciplined the contributors are in separating threads of discussions with new subject headers. Too many spaces with little in them will be disappointing but with too few topics, and a lack of discipline about threading, and they become a mess that no-one can navigate

3   Scheduling and progression over time. How many tasks should there be per week or per month? How do tasks lead from one to another? What will be the pace of discussion? How many messages written per person per week do you expect? How often are students required to login? What will you do about non-

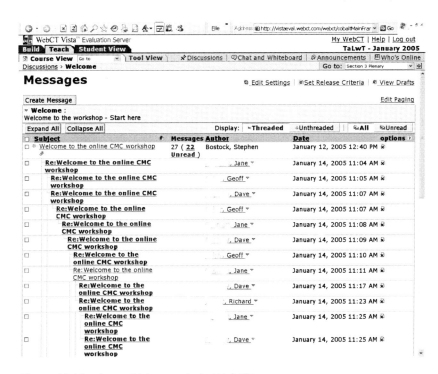

Figure 18 Headers within a topic in WebCT

attendance or about some students 'lurking' (reading but not writing messages)? If you are guessing, on a campus-based course with simple tasks, try a new task every two weeks

4 To assess or not to assess? According to constructive alignment theory (Biggs, 2003), the assessment, intended learning outcomes, and online teaching-learning activities need to be aligned, or congruent. Otherwise, students rightly concentrate on what is assessed, not what they are asked to do. Online activities should either be explicitly assessed - a big advantage is that a full record is kept - or they should be clearly linked to, and benefit students in, later assessment

5 As the online teacher ('moderator') how much do you intend, or are you prepared, to intervene? Will you move or delete messages that are inappropriate? Will you guide or summarise discussions? Monitor but not lead discussions? Use private e-mail to individuals to restrain or encourage them in discussions? Decide in advance and tell the students.

The teaching-learning activities in an online course should develop from the simple to the more ambitious. Salmon (2002) describes this idea as a five stage model:

1 Initial access and motivation by your welcome and encouragement

2 Socialisation of students, familiarising with the online environment and building bridges between cultural, social and learning environments

3 Information exchange, when you support their use of learning materials

4 Knowledge construction by participants, facilitated by you

5 Personal development, supported by you.

Not every course need follow this plan exactly, or reach stage 5 (Lisewski and Joyce, 2003), but having some plan involving a progression is important: *'It is clear that the design of dialogue structures is important, as are the skills of tutors and student participants'* (Webb *et al.*, 2004, p.101); *'Opportunities for reflection need to be built into the design of online conferences'* (Salmon, G., 2002, p.379). At the start, you need to inform students of the design, your intentions and your expectations of them. If designing the whole online activity seems too complex, don't worry. Although you need an initial plan, it can be flexible: you can create or close the spaces and tasks as the course progresses so, to some extent, you can adapt the online environment to student behaviour.

Being an online teacher/facilitator requires new skills for a teacher (Hughes and Daykin, 2002). Online, you have less 'presence' in what is inherently a more democratic situation. There is no easy control of turn-taking. Students won't know how often you or others are

present (although, as the tutor, your discussion software probably allows you to monitor student activity). To begin with you need to keep a close eye on activity. A discussion may take off in its own direction before you notice it. Conversely you may have difficulty getting any contributions. As with all text communication, voice and non-verbal signs are lost: misunderstandings are more likely and can escalate quickly. Therefore, be extra careful to be clear, supportive and business-like. Humour is risky; be sure it cannot be misunderstood. Warn your students of the difficulties of text communication and set the norms for the tone of messages: clear, helpful and polite. Conventionally, online etiquette is called *netiquette*.

Just as in face-to-face teaching, students will vary in their degree of engagement with online discussions depending on their cognitive styles (Cunnigham-Atkins *et al.*, 2004), preferences, experience and abilities (Bostock and Wu Lizhi, 2005).

A wiki is a group-authored Web site. While a blog allows one author to create and develop a Web page without the need for technical skills or a Web authoring tool, a wiki Web site provides similar facilities for a group to create a Web of multiple pages. The Wikipedia (http://en.wikipedia.org), an online encyclopedia, is a good example of a public wiki. Wikis that are private to a student group, for example within a VLE, could be used to jointly author an assignment, or share information relevant to the course. In case a wiki gains an unhelpful contribution, the user's view of it can be 'rolled back' to an earlier state in its history. A wiki is like a Web discussion board in that it is viewed through a browser but different in that it appears as a conventional Web site of linked documents.

6.2   Real-time communication

Text 'chat' is any synchronous text messaging (in real-time) between two or more participants at their own PCs. It is provided by various Web services including VLEs, MSN Messenger, and portals like Yahoo. The text typed by one person is seen by the other(s) as soon as they send it. Messages are typically one line and conversations proceed much faster than in conferencing. It is more like a telephone conversation than like e-mail. The synchronicity may allow spontaneity but, because students have less time to re-read messages and think about their own contributions, the educational quality is likely to be thinner. Participation in an online chat 'room' is either by invitation or by membership of a defined group, such as a course cohort within a VLE. Some software allows the tutor to control students' turn-taking and voting.

Sharing graphics in real time can be accomplished, alongside text chat, with a shared 'electronic whiteboard' (nothing to do with the physical 'interactive whiteboard' discussed in 2.3). All the participants can see and draw on the same white rectangle within a browser window. Although this sounds fun, it is much more demanding on the server and the network connections than text, so it may not be smooth.

Audio- or video-conferencing between two or more participants is also possible, for example with the free Windows MSN. Obviously, the PCs would need microphones, speakers or headphones, and Webcams installed, which would involve technical support for students' own computers. Macromedia Breeze, for example, combines PowerPoint presentations with conferencing using video, audio or text chat.

Unlike asynchronous conferencing, these synchronous technologies require scheduling for synchronous presence. They are more likely to be of use in distance courses than in a campus course alongside onsite activities. Nonetheless, VLEs usually have a 'who's online' feature so that serendipitous online encounters are possible; as a teacher you can hide your online presence to prevent interruptions.

6.3 m-Learning

Not that we need yet another label for learning, but it is worth noting the growth of mobile technologies leading to new possibilities of 'mobile e-learning'. There is an ever increasing variety of mobile devices. At the large end of the spectrum, students can use their full-function laptop PCs connected through wireless networks (e.g. McVay, Snyder and Graez, 2005). At the small end, for example, mobile phones and iPods, there are intrinsic limitations of size and compromises with the user interface - the pointers, keyboards and screens (e.g. Waycott, 2002). In the middle there are various Personal Digital Assistants and 'ultramobile PCs' without full keyboards but with considerable software functionality and connectivity.

As telephony, TV and radio broadcasting, and recorded audio and video all become digital, so it is possible, in different combinations and in ever-smaller devices, to integrate a wide range of functions: audio and video phones and messaging; e-mail and Web access; image/audio/video players; still and video cameras and audio recorders; radio and TV digital broadcasts; Internet broadcasts and podcasts; diaries and organisers; PC application software; handwriting and voice recognition; and GPS (satellite) navigation. Processing ability, storage capacity and battery life, and the connections to wireless phone networks and the Internet, improve relentlessly, widening the range of functions possible in each device.

Are these gadgets just for geeks (those fascinated by technology)? Not necessarily. They could allow students to engage with your course whenever and wherever they wish, suiting their lifestyle (probably rather different from yours). For example, they could download learning

resources or read and write e-mail on their mobile phones, audio players (iPods, MP3 players), laptops or handheld computers. As most students have mobile phones, you could send them text or audio messages to advise them of schedule changes, the availability of library books or learning resources, or reminders of coursework deadlines. Phones could, for example, support teacher assessment, self assessment, and the uploading of messages into a Web-based portfolio (McGuire, 2005), or course evaluation by students (Heppell, 2006). In future, we can expect that VLEs will support such mobile facilities. As these technologies develop, we can look for opportunities for using small mobile devices to support learning: 'Many [teachers] have stated that they are invaluable, improve [student] efficiency and self confidence, are always available, and can be used for a variety of sometimes unexpected purposes' (Robertson et al., 1997, p.188).

6.4 Student peer assessment

'...peer and self assessment are extremely useful in helping students reach their learning goals' (Orsmond, Merry and Callaghan, 2004, p.273)

The ability for 'lifelong learning' involves the ability to make and receive assessments, and this needs practice. There are a number of potential benefits to students of peer assessment. For example, students can assess drafts or intermediate products of a coursework assignment, against specific criteria. By assessing the work of their peers they *use* the assessment criteria and thus understand them better. This will help their self assessment and improvement of their own work. As authors, they will receive feedback from (several of) their peers against the criteria. Understanding the criteria is essential to the process and an important outcome (Liu and Tsai, 2005). Ideally, both assessors and authors should be anonymous to other students as they are uncomfortable giving criticism to peers. On the other hand, while the value of the assessing experience is appreciated by students, they may resent the time taken doing many of them.

For teachers, there is the benefit of students each receiving several times more feedback than the teacher could provide. Of course, each assessment may not be as expert as a teacher's and some students may be unhappy with the quality of some feedback they receive. Multiple assessors will help this, as will explicit and detailed criteria. However, there is a significant administrative task in arranging several anonymous peer assessments for each piece of student work, whether on paper or by e-mail. With 50 students and five assessors for each assignment, this might be 500 e-mails or paper messages for the teacher. What is needed is a Web-based system that accepts student submissions and allows reviewers to download them and submit comments, while maintaining anonymity. For example, the Turnitin service that provides plagiarism detection

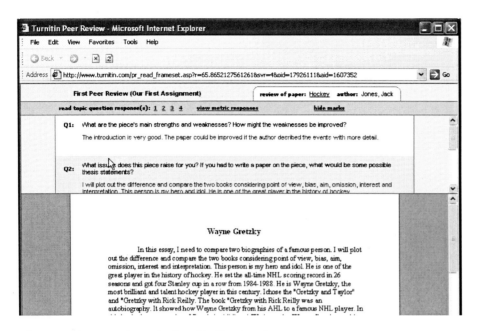

Figure 19 A screen from the Turnitin Peer Review demonstration showing comments on an essay from another student

(http://www.submit.ac.uk) also provides a Web-based service for administering anonymous peer assessment. Teachers can create assessments and their criteria, and specify the assessment process. Student assessors can access certain works and submit their assessments of them anonymously, which are then made accessible to their authors through the Web site (Figure 19). Some researchers have built their own (Bostock, 2002b, Davies, 2000, 2004).

6.5 Further reading

About online discussion

Harris, R. (1999) 'Computer conferencing issues in Higher Education', *Innovations in Education and Training International*, 36 (1): 80-91.

Higgison, C. A. (ed.) (2002) *Online Tutoring e-book from the Online Tutoring Skills* (OTiS) Project, http://otis.scotcit.ac.uk/onlinebook/

Paulsen, M. F. (1995) *The online report on pedagogical techniques for Computer-Mediated Communication*, http://www.nettskolen.com/pub/artikkel.xsql?artid=123

Salmon, G. (2002) *E-tivities*, London: RoutledgeFalmer.

On synchronous chat

Kirkpatrick, G. (2005) 'Online 'chat' facilities as pedagogic tools', *Active Learning in Higher Education*, 6 (2): 145-159.

On mobile learning

http://www.m-learning.org/

Innovative Practice with e-Learning is 'a guide for managers and practitioners in further and higher education on emerging practice with mobile and wireless learning', it says on: http://www.elearning.ac.uk/innoprac/

On PDP

Higher Education Academy, Personal Development Planning, http://www.heacademy.ac.uk/PDP.htm

On netiquette

One description is at http://www.albury.net.au/new-users/netiquet.htm

On videoconferencing

Pitcher, N., Davidson, K. and Goldfinch, J. (2000) 'Videoconferencing in Higher Education', *Innovations in Education and Teaching International*, 37 (3): 199-209.

7 Virtual Learning Environments

This chapter discusses integrated online learning management software, known in the UK as virtual learning environments (VLEs).

7.1 Integrated learning environments

'A Virtual Learning Environment is a Web-based online environment that integrates tools for content delivery, communication, assessment, and student management'
(Littlejohn and Higginson, 2003).

In other words, a VLE provides a toolkit of online services with which a teacher can design and teach a course, whether wholly online or blended with face-to-face meetings. VLEs typically provide the following functions:

1   A space for learning resources, like documents, presentation files and multimedia files, to be uploaded from a teacher's PC or linked to a shared repository. Blogs and wikis allow individual students and groups to add Web content, as well as being able to upload files and assignments

2   Asynchronous text discussions and synchronous text chat

3   Testing, quizzing, evaluation forms, and online assignment submission

4   Selective release of course components, based on time or individual student activity

5   The easy organisation of student groups

6   A grade book linked to central student records

7   Activity tracking of the use of resources, of cohorts and of individuals

8   A calendar, announcements, and other utilities

9   Course-based access derived from central student records, password controlled, and from anywhere at anytime.

A special Web server, with a database, provides all these services, producing Web pages 'on the fly', and differently for every user. The pages are viewed in a Web browser, possibly with the need for the Java environment on the PC. Such an integrated toolkit has advantages for teachers and students compared to using separate software for similar functions: consistency in the user interface and integration between the functions. Most of those functions in current VLEs have been discussed above; this chapter discusses the additional features that integration can support. No doubt VLEs will have further facilities in the near future such as support for peer assessment, e-portfolios and mobile devices.

By 2005, 95% of HEIs and 86% of FEIs had a VLE. The trend is away from individual online services and local systems (for example, for CAA or discussion boards) and towards central systems integrated with, or within,

a VLE. The commercial products Blackboard and WebCT are the commonest VLEs (now one company). In-house software is in decline and free, 'open source' software such as Moodle is on the increase (JISC, 2005).

VLEs increase in educational value as they are integrated into other institutional information systems, including central student records (for populating VLE course spaces accurately and transferring VLE grade book marks), the electronic components of the library, and room bookings and timetabling to provide individual timetables in the VLE calendar and announcements. This wider network of information systems has been labeled a managed learning environment (MLE).

7.2 Roles within a VLE

VLEs support a wider range of roles than those of author (teacher) and user (student) in the use of a plain Web server. The teacher role (sometimes termed *instructor*) gives you the ability to manage online discussions, monitor student activity, and mark assignments, amongst other things. As the author (or *designer*) of a VLE course space (or *section*), you can create or add documents, tests, discussion topics, and other components. The student role generally allows only the use of these components, but may allow uploading of documents within discussions or special folders. A typical teacher in sole control of their course would have roles of designer and instructor, with the ability to see the student view as well. Other roles in some systems are *teaching assistant*, with fewer rights than an instructor, and *auditor*, with read-only access, which could be useful for an external examiner or teaching colleagues, for example. Any role can have multiple individuals using it. The rights of each role are configurable, in a hierarchy of roles with the institution system administrator at the top.

7.3 Integration

For students using more than one online function, the common user interface within a VLE improves learnability - different functions look similar, appear within a common visual framework, and are accessed at the same address. For students, a VLE is easy to use. Their 'home page' within the VLE (e.g. Figure 20) shows them links to the courses on which they are registered, with icons indicating new (to them) items within each course. A calendar shows their composite schedule across courses. Institutional bookmarks can link to important Web sites such as study support and regulations. They can use a *To Do* list and see who else is currently online in their courses so that they can invite them for a synchronous text chat.

For teachers who are designing a VLE space for their course, there are the same advantages of learnability over using separate systems for different functions.

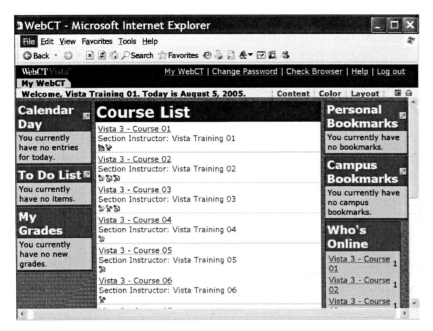

Figure 20 A MyWebCT page

However, the designer/author view is much more complex than that of the student user; there are many more options to choose from. While students with basic IT skills need little or no training, online teachers and designers need significant training.

The integration of the VLE with other systems within the institution can increase the quality of the online experience for teachers and students. Integration with central student records is essential for maintaining the student registrations on the VLE spaces. A common problem at the start of a course is having an accurate list of the students registered on it, who should have access rights to the course VLE space. Your late arrivals may experience problems.

Integration with your online library catalogue, and electronic books or journals to which the library gives access, allows you to provide access to electronic learning resources with a click. Integration of the VLE course grade book (assessment records) with central student records can allow automatic transfer of grades. While this can save the work and errors of re-typing, the transfer must be integrated with the normal assessment procedures.

There is a price to be paid for all this integration and consistency (apart from a hefty license fee): in each functional area (like online assessment) the functionality may not be as powerful or flexible as in 'best of breed' software (like QuestionMark Perception). However, it may be possible to integrate these with your institutional VLE. VLEs can also integrate with information services outside your institution. One candidate is the JISC Plagiarism Detection Service (see 5.3), so that separate submission of work to the PDS Web site would be unnecessary and plagiarism checking could become routine.

7.4 Activity monitoring

A VLE server keeps a detailed record of the activity of all users. Some of the information about students' activities is available to their online teachers. For example, a report may give, for every student, their first and last login time, the number of times they have accessed every online component of the course, and the number of messages they have written and read.

Why would you want to know this detailed information? Some teachers may feel uncomfortable 'spying' on their student's activity. After all (in HE), they are adults and we are encouraging their development as autonomous learners. On the other hand, some students may be having difficulties but not asking for help. Some may be dropping out. Attendance tracking is the rule in FE. On the other hand, one third of HEIs do not track attendance, and even where they do it rarely leads to teaching staff intervening. However, the trend is towards increased attendance tracking, online and onsite, and increased intervention (JISC, 2005). This may be part of the increased attention to 'retention' of students (and their fees). As long as students are told what information can be seen and why it might be used, activity monitoring can be regarded as part of the academic support system. It has its limitations. The data are basically only keyboard and mouse activity - a student may have gone to make a coffee, or be playing an online game in one screen window while making occasional clicks in a VLE to look at your lecture notes! On the other hand, if a student has never logged into your course space, there is clearly a problem.

VLEs also provide reports on the use of each component in your course space. This is useful information when evaluating your course, while it runs or afterwards.

7.5 Communication and groups

In addition to e-mail (chapter 5.1), discussion boards and chat (chapter 6), VLEs also support online announcements and a calendar. Announcements are made by teachers to members of a course, for example. These will appear on the students' VLE home pages and may pop-up in a new browser window to gain attention, although this can be unhelpful for students with some disabilities.

Often, a large student cohort will be divided into smaller groups, for example, for discussions or collaborative work. VLEs provide ways of quickly creating online student groups: at random, or hand-picked, or by the students signing up to groups working on different topics. Once groups are established, they can be used as the targets for the selective release of resources, e-mails, or discussion topics, for example.

7.6 Selective release

Teachers, in a VLE designer role, can specify the conditions for releasing any resource, assessment or activity based on, for example, date and time, or membership of a student group, or grades in the grade book. This selective release facility means that individual students can have a personalised experience based on their activity. For example, certain resources may only become visible once a multiple choice test is passed or a survey questionnaire completed.

Although not essential, VLEs have ways of packaging the resources on a topic into chunks (learning objects). For example, a learning object could be created (by a teacher) to include the documents, assessments and activities related to one topic, which would then be accessed through a menu within that learning object. This 'chunking' makes it easier for teachers to selectively release them, re-use them and share them, and makes it easier for students to navigate the course.

7.7 Integrating online and onsite environments

Course design should integrate technology and face-to-face activity around the student experience, so that it is experienced by students as educationally coherent, or aligned, with the other course components, particularly with assessment and intended learning outcomes (e.g. Hall, 2002). Technology should be experienced as embedded, not bolted on. VLEs offer integration of the online aspects of a course and multimedia consoles and multimedia consoles and IWBs offer integration of the technologies supporting face-to-face teaching. We must also integrate online and onsite teaching-learning activities. For example, the online aspects of a course could be discussed in advance, face-to-face. Later, in a technology-supported classroom, the online discussions could be reviewed on the large screen, and be made the subject of face-to-face discussions or other activities. Weekly online tasks of reading and writing could prime students for their face-to-face tutorials, thus improving the discussion in them (Duco van Oostrum, 2006, personal communication).

Conversely, the products of face-to-face discussions could be added to the online resources, and be particularly helpful to those who were not present. You can easily put electronic presentation slides and electronic flipcharts into a VLE space. Students could be asked to take minutes of small-group discussions to upload to the VLE afterwards, as an alternative to you running a plenary discussion with a large group. Digital photographs of larger pieces of non-electronic work can be added to the online course resources. You could make electronic records of lectures (audio or video or multimedia) available online, if that would be useful for student learning, although I would prefer to integrate student online activities within those in interactive lectures or tutorials. If a face-to-face session takes place in a room equipped with networked PCs, or where students have laptops connected through a wireless network, online and onsite work can be seamless. Designing courses which integrate (or blend) technology into the course is the subject of the next chapter.

7.8 Further reading

The JISC (Joint Information Systems Committee) Web includes 22 briefing papers on VLEs and MLEs. Start with *MLEs and VLEs explained*, http://www.jisc.ac.uk/index.cfm?name=mle_briefings_1

A description of VLEs in general is at http://www.jisc.ac.uk/uploaded_documents/req-vle.doc

Bostock, S. J. (2003) 'VLEs - Don't panic!', *Educational Developments* 4.4, p.28, http://www.keele.ac.uk/depts/aa/landt/lt/docs/vles-dont-panic.htm

Joint Information Systems Committee (2005) *Study of Environments to Support E-learning in UK Further and Higher Education*, http://www.jisc.ac.uk/uploaded_documents/ e-learning_survey_2005.pdf

Coventry University VLE Web site, http://home.ched.coventry.ac.uk/course/vlehome.html

8 Designing blended learning

This chapter is different: it is not about types of technology and their uses, nor is it in the organiser in Chapter 1. Instead, it provides some ideas about how you might go about *systematically* designing technology into a course. It is aimed at the middle of the scale of curriculum development: not at whole programmes taught by teams and not at individual lesson plans, but at the individual semester course or module.

If you are part of an institutional or departmental initiative to change your pedagogy (e.g. adopt problem-based learning) or adopt a technology (e.g. online quizzes for feedback), some course design decisions already have been made. Nonetheless, the discussions in previous chapters of the affordances and constraints of the different technologies should help you decide how to use them, and the discussion below of the criteria for selecting technologies may help you refine your design.

8.1 Getting started

If you just read the whole of this book (well done!), you may be feeling overwhelmed by the educational possibilities of technology. What to use and how to plan the integration? If you are starting from an existing course, the simplest way to start is by listing its problems (all courses have them) and the opportunities technology seems to present to improve the experience for your students or yourself. However, while this approach may produce a useful improvement, we can adopt a more systematic one.

In any development project we normally precede design decisions with an analysis stage, describing the factors in the situation likely to affect our design (Bostock, 2003, 2006; JISC, 2004). A checklist of factors is:

1   Your teaching philosophy and style - if possible, you want to design a course you enjoy teaching

2   The learners, who they are, what they already know, their abilities and their learning styles

3   Other stakeholders including colleagues, your department and institution e.g. its regulations or learning and teaching strategy

4   The subject domain and the intended learning outcomes for the learners

5   The learning environment, including the onsite and online resources available to you, and any constraints e.g. timetabling or online access.

We are often so immersed in our teaching situations that we know all the above tacitly, but it is worth writing it down to consider again. Finally, it is not too early to think about evaluation: your criteria for success and what evaluation methods you will use to assess that.

8.2 Constructive alignment by blending

The design method that follows has three assumptions. Firstly, the curriculum is outcomes-based. Intended learning outcomes could include subject specific knowledge; subject specific skills; cognitive skills e.g. critical analysis; and so-called key skills e.g. use of IT (QAA, 1999). Although there are critiques of outcomes-based design (e.g. Barnett and Coate, 2005), it is the dominant assumption in the UK and it demands a certain clarity of intention that is helpful.

Secondly, students must construct their own knowledge and they do so by performing the teaching-learning activities and assessments we design.

Thirdly, teaching, learning and assessment (*i.e.* summative grading) must be integrated. In particular, both assessment and teaching-learning activities should be driven by the intended learning outcomes. *Constructive alignment* (Biggs, 2003) is an influential model that combines the second assumption of individual knowledge construction (*constructive*) with the design of teaching and assessment driven by the intended learning outcomes (*alignment*).

Blended learning design is an example of constructive alignment where some TLAs or assessments are technology-based. The principle is unchanged: teaching, learning, and assessment, both online and onsite, are aligned with intended outcomes. The ideal is the mutual support of these course components. The uses of technology-based components should be supportive of other teaching/learning/assessment activities; online supporting offline, and *vice versa* (see 7.7). Finally, for campus universities, an optimal experience for both teacher and students would be a balanced blend of technology-based and traditional TLAs, within the teaching and learning hours available. (Who wants to spend all day reading and writing e-mails, however effective they are?) Some variety in online and offline activities will address the variety of students. If technology is used in aligned, mutually supportive and balanced ways, it should become permanently embedded and valued.

To these assumptions we could add the principle that using technology should empower students, expanding the opportunities for learning, not creating barriers for any students.

Moving now to the design decisions, we first need to generate some options and then select those that will constitute our intended blend. Figure 21 is a table that could be used to generate possible online and onsite teaching-learning activities (TLAs) and assessments (printable versions of these forms can be found at http://www.e-t.org.uk).

Assessment tasks – online (CAA)	Assessment tasks – onsite/ traditional	Intended learning outcomes	TLAs online	TLAs onsite
		1		
		2		
		3		
		4		

Figure 21 Generating options for assessment and TLAs consistent with intended learning outcomes

Starting with writing (or accepting) the intended learning outcomes, we list them in the centre column. For each ILO we can imagine one or more possible TLAs and assessment tasks, both online and onsite. To deal with just the right-hand columns for TLAs, Figure 22 is a notional example of a course with four ILOs. Once the options have been recorded the crucial design decision amounts to selecting one or more options for each ILO. In this example it might be the choice made in Figure 23. ILO 1 is supported by both online and onsite TLAs, and the other ILOs use either online or onsite support.

	ILO	Online TLA options	Onsite TLA options
1	Recall information W	Web documents and links	Reading a set book, lectures
2	Perform skill X	Formative quizzes	Problem sheets in class
3	Contribute to discussion on Y	Asynchronous text discussions	Tutorials
4	Apply knowledge and skills to Z	Computer simulation	A field trip

Figure 22 A notional example of TLA options

	ILO	Online TLA	Onsite TLA
1	Recall information W	Web documents and links	Reading a set book, lectures
2	Perform skill X		Problem sheets in class
3	Contribute to discussion on Y	Asynchronous text discussions	
4	Apply knowledge and skills to Z		A field trip

Figure 23 A blended selection for the notional example

Assessment tasks – online (CAA)	Assessment tasks – onsite/ traditional	Intended learning outcomes	TLAs online	TLAs onsite
MCQ quizzes		1 Recall W	Web documents and links	Reading a set book, lectures
	Problems in a closed examination	2 Perform X		Problem sheets in class
Assessed asynchronous text discussion		3 Discuss Y	Asynchronous text discussion	
	Field notebook	4 Apply Z		A field trip

Figure 24 A blended design of TLAs and assessments

Having identified possible options for online and onsite TLAs (and, later, for assessments), how are we to make the selection? A first pass can be achieved by considering three broad strategies:

Deficit – technology provides missing support for learning activities, e.g. online discussion in distance learning

Substitution – substitute a traditional element with a technology-based one, e.g. online tutorials replace onsite tutorials

Enrichment – technology duplicates existing TLAs, giving a choice of media suitable for different learning styles, e.g. lecture handouts on web, podcasts.

The tables imply a simplification in many cases: ILOs, TLAs and assessments do not necessarily have a one-to-one relationship, but this can be indicated on the tables. After conducting a similar process of option generation and selection of assessments, we could get a final design such as Figure 24.

8.3 Efficiency and effectiveness

We can now consider further the selection criteria of efficiency and effectiveness. Effectiveness is ultimately the learners' achievement of the intended outcomes, and possibly of additional unexpected benefits. At the time of making the design decision, this will be based on the teacher's judgement; later it can be informed by the students' evaluation of the learning experience and by the assessment outcomes.

Efficiency is the ratio of outputs (students passing the course) to inputs (costs), which may be important if student numbers were to increase or costs need to be reduced. Typically, in my experience, the marginal costs for a course are mostly academic staff time: preparing and performing the teaching and assessment. Many innovations in e-learning have been successful only because of the extra, unpaid time the teachers have devoted. This is not sustainable and not helpful to designing embedded learning technology. Teaching workload should not be increased because of using technology; if anything it should be decreased. Some uses of technology may require an additional up-front development cost in time but you must be confident you can recoup it within a few years.

The time costs to students must also not increase. Their learning hours are fixed for each course, in relation to the credits it generates. (At my institution, there are 150 learning hours for a typical semester course.) Designing technology into a course must not increase the time expected of students over that allotted for the course.

To help with designing within these time constraints the table used above can be expanded to record the hours involved in different options for both teacher and learner (Figure 25). When a blended selection of online and onsite TLAs has been made the hours involved can be

ILOs	TLA online	TLA onsite	Teacher time		Learner time	
			Online	Onsite	Online	Onsite
1						
2						
3						
4						
Total of hours:						

Figure 25 Checking time costs of a blend of TLAs

totalled to check they are within those available for teacher and learner.

A similar structure can be used for designing a mix of online (CAA) and onsite (traditional) assessments (Figure 26). Effectiveness criteria here are the validity of the testing of outcomes, the reliability of the result, and the utility in terms of motivational effects on learning. Efficiency is mostly, again, about time costs, in assessment preparation (staff setting assessment tasks and student revision) and performance (student time to complete assessment and staff marking). Again, the total times, when added to those for TLAs, must not exceed the time properly available. A sober consideration of

time costs may cause a rethink of an initial selection of TLAs or of assessments; design is usually an iterative process.

This chapter has suggested a way of selecting a blend of TLAs and assessments, consistent with the constructive alignment model of teaching and learning. Other educational assumptions could replace ILOs as the driver of curriculum integration. The generation of teaching, learning and assessment options, both online and onsite, and the subsequent selection of a mix of these, could still be used as a systematic design method. That, however, is for a different discussion.

ILOs	CAA: Online assessment	CAA: Online assessment	Teacher time		Learner time	
			Online	Onsite	Online	Onsite
1						
2						
3						
4						
Total of hours:						

Figure 26 Checking time costs of a blend of assessments

8.4 Further reading

The support web for this book has copies of these tools for printing.

http://www.e-t.org.uk

The Joint Information Systems Committee (JISC) is funding a large project, *e-Learning and Pedagogy*, with many useful reports.

http://www.jisc.ac.uk/index.cfm?name=elearning_pedagogy

Boyle, T. (1997) *Design for multimedia learning*, Hemel Hempstead: Prentice Hall.

This has a section on educational design including constructivism.

The Embedding Learning Technologies Web has links to course materials.

http://www.elt.ac.uk

Thorne, K. (2003) *Blended learning: how to integrate online and traditional learning*, New Jersey: Kogan Page.

Dalgarno, B. (2001) 'Interpretations of constructivism and consequences for Computer Assisted Learning', *British Journal of Educational Technology*, 32 (2): 183-194.

(All Web sites accessed on 29 June 2006)

References

Alonso, F., López, G., Manrique, D. and Viñes, J. (2005) 'An instructional model for Web-based e-learning education with a blended learning process approach', *British Journal of Educational Technology*, 36 (2): 217-235.

Anderson, T. (1997) 'Integrating lectures and electronic course materials', *Innovations in Education and Training International* 34 (1): 24-31.

Andreson, L. (1990) 'Lecturing to large groups', in Rust, C. (ed.) *Teaching in Higher Education*, SCED Paper 57.

Baldwin, L. and Sabry, K. (2003) 'Learning styles for interactive learning systems', *Innovations in Education and Teaching International*, 40 (4): 325-340.

Barford, J. and Weston, C. (1997) 'The use of video as a teaching resource', *British Journal of Educational Technology*, 28 (1): 40-50.

Barnett, R. and Coate, K. (2005) *Engaging the curriculum in Higher Education*, Buckingham: SRHE and OU Press.

Biggs, J. (2003) *Teaching for quality learning at university*, 2nd edition, Buckingham: SRHE and OU Press.

Bligh, D. (1998) *What's the use of lectures?*, 5th edition, Exeter: Intellect.

Bloom, B. S. (1956) *Taxonomy of educational objectives, Handbook 1: Cognitive domain*, London: Longmans Green and Co.

Bostock, S. J. (1996) 'A critical review of Laurillard's classification of educational media', *Instructional Science*, 24: 71-88.

Bostock, S. J. (1998) 'Constructivism in Mass Higher Education: a Case Study', *British Journal of Educational Technology*, 29 (3): 225-240. (The course referred to is archived at www.keele.ac.uk/depts/aa/landt/lt/Internet/subinprg.htm)

Bostock, S. J. (2001) 'Online resources to help students evaluate online resources', *Educational Developments*, 2.2: 15. www.keele.ac.uk/depts/aa/landt/lt/docs/webevaluations.htm

Bostock, S. J. (2002) 'Designing Web sites that are accessible to all', *Educational Developments*, 3.3: 18-19.

Bostock, S. J. (2002b) *Web Support for Student Peer Review*, Keele University Innovation Project Report, item 1 on www.keele.ac.uk/depts/aa/landt//projects/index.htm, accessed 23 December 2005.

Bostock, S. J. (2003) 'Learning technologies: Review and Needs Analysis', a workshop organised by the EFFECTS TLTP3 project at the LSE, London, 26 February.

Bostock, S. J. (2004) 'Motivation and electronic assessment', pp.86-99, chapter 9, in Irons, A. and Alexander, S. (eds) *Effective Learning and Teaching in Computing*, Routledge Falmer: London.

Bostock, S. J. (2005) 'Editorial', *Educational Developments* 6.2: 6.

Bostock, S. J. (2005b) 'Embedding Learning Technologies', pp.6-9, *SEDA-PDF: The SEDA Professional Development Framework*, Birmingham: SEDA.

Bostock, S. J. (2006) *Practitioner tools for designing blended learning*, a presentation at the First Annual Blended Learning Conference: Blended Learning — Promoting Dialogue in Innovation and Practice, University of Hertfordshire, 15th June.

Bostock, S. J., Hulme, J. A. and Davys, M. A. (2006) 'CommuniCubes: Intermediate Technology For Interaction With Student Groups', in Banks, David. (ed.) *Audience Response Systems in Higher Education*, Hershey PA, USA: Idea Group Publishing.

Bostock S. J., Roberts, P., Bashford, L. and Mahon, M. (2005) *Facilitating Problem-Based Learning Using an Interactive Whiteboard*, a presentation at The Association for the Study of Medical Education, Annual Scientific Meeting, 11-13 July, Newcastle.

Bostock, S. J. and Wu Lizhi (2005) 'Gender in Student Online Discussions', *Innovations in Education and Teaching International*, 42 (1): 73-86.

Boyle, J. T. and Nicol, D. J. (2003) 'Using classroom communication systems to support interaction and discussion in large class settings', *ALT-J*, 11 (3): 43-57.

Brooksbank, D. J., Clark, A., Hamilton, R. and Pickernell, D. G. (1998) 'A critical appraisal of WinEcon and its use in a first year undergraduate Economics programme', *ALT-J*, 6 (3): 47-53.

Bull, J. and McKenna, C. (2003) *A Blueprint for Computer-assisted Assessment*, London: RoutledgeFalmer.

Buzan, T. (1993) *The mind map book*, London: BBC Books.

Chickering, A. W. and Ehrmann, S. C. (1996) *Implementing the seven principles: technology as lever*, www.clt.astate.edu/clthome/Implementing%20the%20seven%20principles,%20ehrmann%20and%20chickering.pdf, accessed 25 November 2005.

Chickering, A. W. and Gamson, Z. (1987) 'Seven principles for good practice', *AAHE Bulletin*, 39: 3-7.

ClickandGo (2002) *Video Streaming: a guide for educational development*, www.clickandgovideo.ac.uk/, accessed 2 August 2005.

Conole, G. (2004) *Report on the effectiveness of tools for e-learning*, www.cetis.ac.uk:8080/pedagogy/research_study/tools%20report%20-%20final.doc, on the JISC e-learning programme, pedagogy community site, accessed 23 December 2005.

CSALT (2001) *Effective networked learning in higher education: notes and guidelines*, http://csalt.lancs.ac.uk/jisc/, accessed 27 December 2005.

Cunningham-Atkins, H., Powell, N., Moore, D., Hobbs, D. and Sharpe, S. (2004) 'The role of cognitive style in educational computer conferencing', *British Journal of Educational Technology*, 35 (1): 69-80.

Davies, P. (2000) 'Computerized Peer Assessment', *Innovations in Education and Training International*, 37 (4): 346-355.

Davies, P. (2003) *Practical Ideas for Enhancing Lectures*, SEDA Special 13, Birmingham: SEDA.

Davies, P. (2004) 'Don't write, just mark: the validity of assessing student ability via their computerized peer-marking of an essay rather than the creation of an essay', *ALT-J*, 12 (3): 261-277.

Draper, S.W. and Brown, M.I. (2004) 'Increasing interactivity in lectures using an electronic voting system', *Journal of Computer Assisted Learning*, 20: 81-94.

Falchikov, N. (2003) 'Involving students in assessment', *Psychology Learning and Teaching,* 3 (2): 102-108.

Fillion, G., Limayem, M. and Bouchard, L. (1999) 'Videoconferencing in distance education: a study of student perceptions in the lecture context', *Innovations in Education and Training International,* 36 (4): 302-319.

Ford, N. and Chen, S. Y. (2001) 'Matching/mismatching revisited: an empirical study of learning and teaching styles', *British Journal of Educational Technology,* 32 (1): 5-22.

Freeman, M. (1998) 'Video conferencing: a solution to the multi-campus large classes problem?', *British Journal of Educational Technology,* 29 (3): 197-210.

Gedalof, A. J. (1998) *Teaching large classes* (Green Guide 1), Halifax, Canada: STLHE.

Grabinger, R. S. and Dunlap, J. C. (1995) 'Rich Environments for Active Learning', *ALT-J,* 3 (2): 5-34.

Griffiths, J. R. and Brophy, P. (2002) *Student searching behaviour in the JISC Information Environment,* Ariadne, Issue 33, www.ariadne.ac.uk/issue33/edner/intro.html, accessed 27 December 2005.

Hall, R. (2002) 'Aligning learning, teaching and assessment using the Web: an evaluation of pedagogic approaches', *British Journal of Educational Technology,* 33 (2): 149-158.

HEFCE (2003) *Intellectual property rights in e-Learning programmes: a good practice guide,* www.hefce.ac.uk/pubs/hefce/2003/03_08.htm, accessed 23 December 2005.

Hegarty, J. R., Bostock, S. J. and Collins, D. (2000) 'Staff development in information technology for special needs: a new, distance-learning course at Keele University', *British Journal of Educational Technology,* 31 (3): 199-212.

Heppell, S. (2006) 'Innovation right under your nose', *Education Guardian,* June 20, p.6.

Higher Education Academy (2002) *Guide to Curriculum Design: Personal Development Planning,* www.heacademy.ac.uk/843.htm, accessed 27 December 2005.

Hughes, M. and Daykin, N. (2002) 'Towards constructivism: Investigating students' perceptions and learning as a result of using an online environment', *Innovations in Education and Teaching International,* 39 (3): 217-224.

JISC (2004) *Effective Practice Planner,* http://www.jisc.ac.uk/elp_practice.html, accessed 8 June 2006.

JISC (2005) *Study of Environments to Support E-learning in UK Further and Higher Education,* Joint Information Systems Committee, http://www.jisc.ac.uk/uploaded_documents/e-learning_survey_2005.pdf, accessed 23 December 2005.

Johnson, M. I., Dewhurst, D. G. and Williams, A. D. (1997) 'Computer-based interactive tutorial versus traditional lecture for teaching introductory aspects of pain', *ALT-J,* 5 (3): 22-31

Joiner, R., Durkin, C., Morrison, D. and Williams, L. (2003) 'Activating Boxmind: an evaluation of a Web-based video lecture with synchronized activities', *ALT-J,* 11 (3): 19-30.

Kennewell, S. (2001) 'Using affordances and constraints to evaluate the use of information and communications technology in teaching and learning', *Journal of Information Technology for Teacher Education,* 10 (1 and 2): 101-116.

Knight, P. T. (2002) 'Summative Assessment in Higher Education: practices in disarray', *Studies in Higher Education,* 27 (3): 275-286.

Knipe, D. and Lee, M. (2002) 'The quality of teaching and learning via videoconferencing', *British Journal of Educational Technology,* 33 (3): 301-311.

Laurillard, D. (1995) 'Multimedia and the changing experience of the learner', *British Journal of Educational Technology,* 26 (3): 179-189.

Laurillard, D. (2002) *Rethinking University Teaching,* London: Routledge, 2nd edition.

Lisewski, B. and Joyce, P. (2003) 'Examining the five-stage e-moderating model: designed and emergent practice in the learning technology profession', *ALT-J,* 11 (1): 55-66.

Littlejohn, A. and Higginson, C. (2003) *e-Learning series number 3: a guide for teachers,* LTSN Generic Centre, www.heacademy.ac.uk/1682.htm, accessed 27 December 2005.

Liu, C. and Tsai, C. (2005) 'Peer assessment through Web-based knowledge acquisition: tools to support conceptual awareness', *Innovations in Education and Teaching International,* 42 (1): 43-59.

Mayes, J. T. and De Freitas, S. (2004) Review of e-learning theories, frameworks and models, report for JISC, www.jisc.ac.uk/uploaded_documents/stage%202%20learning %20models%20(version%201).pdf, accessed 30 November 2005.

McGuire, L. (2005) 'Assessment using new technology', *Innovations in Education and Teaching International,* 42 (3): 265-276.

McVay, G. J. Snyder, K. D. and Graez, K. A. (2005) 'Evaluation of a laptop university: a case study', *British Journal of Educational Technology,* 36 (3): 513-524.

Meek, J., Garnett, M. and Grattan, J. (1998) 'Evaluating the impact of Internet provision on students' information-gathering strategies', *ALT-J,* 6 (1): 57-63.

Monteith, M. and Smith, J. (2000) 'Learning in a virtual campus: the pedagogical implications of students' experiences', *Innovations in Education and Teaching International,* 38 (2): 119-127.

Moss, J. and Hendry, G. (2002) 'Use of electronic surveys in course evaluation', *British Journal of Educational Technology,* 33 (5): 583-92.

Murray, L., Hourigan, T., Jeanneau, C. and Chappell, D. (2005) 'Netskills and the current state of beliefs and practices in student learning: an assessment and recommendations', *British Journal of Educational Technology,* 36 (3): 425-438.

O'Hagan, C. (1997) *Using varied media to improve communication and learning,* SEDA Special 4, Birmingham: SEDA.

Oliver, M. and Conole, G. (1998) 'A pedagogical framework for embedding C&IT into the curriculum', *ALT-J,* 6 (2): 4-16.

Oliver, M. and Smith, J. (2005) 'Exploring behaviour in the online environment: student perceptions of information literacy', *ALT-J*, 13 (1): 49-65.

Orsmond, P., Merry, S. and Callaghan, A. (2004) 'Implementation of a formative assessment model incorporating peer and self assessment', *Innovations in Education and Teaching International*, 41 (3): 274-290.

Paulsen, M. F. (1995) *The online report on pedagogical techniques for Computer-Mediated Communication*, www.nettskolen.com/pub/artikkel.xsql?artid=123, accessed 2 August 2005.

Peat, M. (2000) 'Online self assessment materials: do these make a difference to student learning?', *ALT-J*, 8 (2): 51-57.

Peat, M. and Franklin, S. (2002) 'Supporting student learning: the use of computer-based formative assessment modules', *British Journal of Educational Technology*, 33 (5): 515-523.

Phillips, S. (2005) 'Lectures that really do click', *Times Higher Education Supplement*, 21 October 2005.

QAA (1999) *Guidelines For Preparing Programme Specifications*, www.qaa.ac.uk/academicinfrastructure/programspec/, accessed 8 June 2006.

QAA (2000) *The framework for higher education qualifications in England, Wales and Northern Ireland*, Quality Assurance Agency for Higher Education (UK).

Riding, R. (1996) *Learning styles and technology-based training*, Sheffield: Department for Education and Employment.

Riding, R. and Grimley, M. (1999) 'Cognitive style, gender and learning from multi-media materials', *British Journal of Educational Technology*, 30 (1): 43-56.

Riding, R. and Rayner, S. (1998) *Cognitive styles and learning strategies: understanding style differences in learning and behaviour*, London: David Fulton.

Robertson, M., Calder, J., Fung, P. and O'Shea, T. (1997) 'The use and effectiveness of palmtop computers in education', *British Journal of Educational Technology*, 28 (3): 177-189.

Russell, E. (2004) *Guidelines on developing a policy for managing e-mail*, www.nationalarchives.gov.uk/electronicrecords/advice/pdf/managing_e-mails.pdf, accessed 7 November 2005.

Salmon, G. (2002) *E-tivities*, London: RoutledgeFalmer.

Salmon, G. (2002) 'Mirror, mirror, on my screen… Exploring online reflections', *British Journal of Educational Technology*, 33 (4): 379-391.

Saunders, G. and Klemming, F. (2003) 'Integrating technology into a traditional learning environment', *Active Learning in Higher Education*, 4 (1): 74-86.

Schott, B. (2006) Schott's Almanac 2006, London: Bloomsbury.

Shephard, K. (2003) 'Questioning, promoting and evaluating the use of streaming video to support student learning', *British Journal of Educational Technology*, 34 (3): 295-308.

Smith, B. (1997) *Lecturing to large groups*, SEDA Special number 1, Birmingham: SEDA.

Smith, K. (2004) '"The opposite of talking isn't listening; it's waiting." Possible criteria for oral assessment, and questions of parity', Chapter 4, Wisker, G. (ed.) *Developing and assessing students' oral skills*, SEDA Special 17, Birmingham: SEDA.

Soper, J. B. and MacDonald, A. B. (1994) 'An interactive approach to learning economics: the Winecon package', *ALT-J*, 2 (1): 14-29.

Swain, H. (2006) 'Look out for the sound argument', *Times Higher Education Supplement*, June 16, p.58.

Teacher Training Agency (1998) *The use of ICT in subject teaching*, London: TTA.

Valley, K. (1997) 'Learning styles and courseware design', *ALT-J*, 5 (2): 42-51.

Walker, J. R. and Taylor, T. (1998) *The Columbia Guide to Online Style*, Columbia UP, summarised at www.columbia.edu/cu/cup/cgos/idx_basic.html, accessed 16 May 2003.

Waycott, J. (2002) 'Reading with new tools: an evaluation of Personal Digital Assistants as tools for reading course materials', *ALT-J*, 10 (2): 38-50.

Webb, E., Jones, A., Barker, P. and van Schaik, P. (2004) 'Using e-learning dialogues in higher education', *Innovations in Education and Teaching International*, 41 (1): 93-103.

Winter, R. (2003) 'Contextualizing the patchwork text: addressing problems of coursework assessment in higher education', *Innovations in Education and Training International*, 40 (2): 112-122.

Wisker, G. (2004) Developing and assessing students' oral skills, Chapter 1 in *SEDA Special 17* of the same name, Birmingham: SEDA.

Index

SEDA Paper 119 – e-Teaching: Engaging Learners Through Technology